How To
Answer
Interview
Questions

© Copyright Peggy McKee, 2017

All rights reserved.

Peggy McKee

About the Author

Peggy McKee is an expert resource and a dedicated advocate for job seekers in every step of the job search process—from resumes to interviews to getting the offer. As CEO of Career Confidential, she educates job seekers, providing strategies and tools for a fast, wildly successful job search. So far, Career Confidential has helped over 23,000 people in 90 countries get hired fast.

Career Confidential's website, http://CareerConfidential.com, offers 100+ products, tools, apps and webinars for job seekers, as well as several e-books. More than 10,000 people attend Career Confidential's free job search and interview webinars every month, and over 1 Million people around the world have downloaded materials. Peggy receives positive responses every day from candidates who have used them to land the job of their ms, and she loves that she's been able to contribute to their s.

Peggy McKee has 15+ years of experience in sales, management, recruiting, and career coaching. In 1999, Peggy founded PHC Consulting, a medical sales recruiting firm. When she consistently found herself offering advice to jobseekers who weren't even her own candidates, she developed a new business model to offer personalized career coaching as well as the tools jobseekers need to thrive and succeed in the job search...and Career Confidential was born. She believes that her experience has led to her unique advice and unparalleled success rate. Recognized as a job search authority, Peggy has been named #1 on the list of the Top 25 Most Influential Online Recruiters by HR Examiner, and has been quoted in articles from CNN, CAP TODAY, Yahoo!HotJobs, and the Denver Examiner.

Contents

Are you overqualified for this job?

If you get asked this question, you may jump straight to frustrated—especially if you're an older worker and assume they're telling you you're just too old. But companies facing hiring issues really don't want to make a mistake. They don't want to go to the time and expense of hiring someone who will just move on to something that pays more as soon as they find it. And most people want to climb the ladder and make more money, so why wouldn't you?

So when they ask you if you have too much experience, think about the question behind the question. What they're really asking is, are you going to be bored? Is this really the right position for you? Are you really going to be satisfied here? Drill down a little more and it's: Are you a good fit for this job?

Answer **that** question. They're looking for you to help them feel better about hiring you. You can do that with the answer you give and believe me, they're listening. They know they can learn a lot about you from what you choose to say.

Here are some suggestions:

"I might be overqualified, but wouldn't that be wonderful for you? Because then you'd have someone who was more than ready to do well in this...someone who's done this before, who understands what it takes to be successful at it and can do it again." Remember, they always need to know the answer to those 4 unasked job interview questions: Do you understand the job? Can you do the job? Will you do the job? Do you pose a risk to their own continued employment?

Or you can say, "The truth is that I am overqualified for the job. But it looks wonderful to me because of X, Y, and Z." X, Y, and Z are your own reasons why this job fits you (other than money or responsibilities or possibility for advancement).

And it could be anything. I remember speaking to one gentleman who was clearly overqualified for the job he was applying for, but who wanted it because the commute was significantly shorter. The company was freaking out because they didn't understand, but he said, "Hey, my house is paid off so I don't need the money, and I like where I live. I'm not interested in moving. I just want to live my life. And right now, my job requires a 2-hour round-trip ordeal every day. I don't want that anymore. This place is 5 minutes from my house. That extra time in my day would be worth a lot to me."

Once he communicated that to them, they understood and were excited about hiring him.

You have to tell them why they're perfect for you. They may not always understand it on their own.

And they will make assumptions about you. You can't just think that they will take you at face value. This is a big risk for them and they want to not make a mistake. So help them see why you're a great fit.

Are you willing to relocate?

Are you willing to move for a new job? In many companies, this is a typical question. Sometimes it's a deal-breaker, sometimes it isn't. Even if this particular job doesn't require it, many companies want that flexibility in their employees for long-term growth potential.

The knee-jerk answer that most people give ("I'd consider it for the right opportunity.") is not your best answer, even if it is the truth. Because it puts your motivation for wanting the job more into the 'money' category rather than the 'fulfilling work / great fit' category. It's a subtle but important distinction, and it will take the shine off your candidacy if you say it.

Here's how to handle the relocation question for several different life circumstances you might be in:

If you're a 'No'
If your answer is unequivocally 'no', you have to say so. It's only going to cause you problems if they do end up offering you

the job and you won't move. (Although, let me just say that if it's "absolutely not", remember that life can turn on a dime. What looks like "never" right now might not look like that in a few months or a year.) If you really want this job, and you can't move immediately, say so. But consider saying something like, "I'd rather not move right now, but you never know what tomorrow will bring. And I'm very interested in this position and this company."

If you're a 'Maybe'

But maybe you feel like there's some wiggle room. You'd rather not commit to packing up your entire life just yet, but you don't want this job to slip through your fingers because of it. It may be that you really don't want to move...the kids are settled, your family is here, and so on...but for the right offer you'd consider it. You know you can't say that, so try something like, "I'm interested in growing my career, and if relocating for the job is a necessary part of that, of course I'd consider it." That doesn't commit you to moving. It just confirms that your career (and this job) is important—and it's tactful.

Or, you could toss it back to them: "Where I live is not the most important issue for me. Utilizing my skills, developing new ones, and advancing my career are really my driving interests, and I've become more and more convinced that this company and this job is a really great fit because of my skills in X, Y, and Z. Do you agree?"

You've stayed on track, selling yourself for the job, and redirected the conversation (hopefully). If they keep pushing, you can fall back to the "of course I'd consider it" statement.

None of these answers commit you to anything. But all of them help you appear to be more sincere, flexible, tactful, and reasonable than "I'd consider it for the right opportunity." They keep the conversation going in a positive direction, which is a big plus for any job interview.

http://careerconfidential.com

Job Interview Question 3

Describe a time when your work was criticized and how you handled it.

Have you ever been asked this question? I know...to you, it feels like oral surgery without the Novocain...but interviewers love behavioral interviews because they tell them so much about you—in the story you choose to tell, how you tell it, with what kind of attitude, and the results you're capable of producing under pressure. They just can't get as good a picture of what life would be like with you on the job from only asking about your skills and qualifications.

The criticism question is one of those **adversity pieces** that you've always got to have a story or two about in your back pocket for interviews.

The truth is, to be a good employee (or an overall successful person), you've always got to be open to criticism. If you're not open to criticism, then you're not coachable. If you're not coachable, then you're less valuable than you could be.

Are you coachable? Coachability is huge. Taking criticism is important. If, when you get criticism, you have a problem with always wanting to be defensive and not simply soaking up how you could have done it differently, then you'll find that people will give you less and less criticism. That might sound like a good thing, but it isn't.

If they can't communicate with you and help you be better (which helps them to be better), they'll eventually just fire you. Does that seem extreme? It's because your boss (or anyone you need to learn something from) can't teach you anything new without correcting you once in a while. Since no one's perfect, everyone needs to be corrected or coached to a new place or behavior in order to keep being successful.

So what they're really looking for is, **are you coachable?** Tell me about a time when someone told you how you could do something different or better, how you did do it different or better, and then what the results were.

This is the **STAR technique** that all job seekers should be familiar with for behavioral interviews. STAR stands for Situation or Task, Action, and Result. Stories put into that structure are particularly effective in job interview situations. You talk about the situation you were in and the task in front of you, the action you choose to take and the results you got from it (what happened). Choose an incident or experience from your work history, put it into that structure, and you've got yourself a story that illustrates why you're such a great pick for the job.

http://careerconfidential.com

Job Interview Question 4

Describe a time when your workload was heavy and how you handled it.

Asking you to describe difficult situations (and your reactions to them) is a favorite tactic of interviewers. It's called behavioral interviewing. Behavioral interview questions get way past your basic skills and qualifications and get to the heart of "how will you act once you're hired?" Past behavior predicts future behavior better than anything else.

The reason you have to be able to speak to this issue in an interview is that they want to know if you're going to freak out when they have a rough time. And everyone eventually has a rough time. Accountants tend to get swamped in March, and retailers at Christmas. But even jobs without a seasonal aspect like those can have times when the workload is particularly stressful.

Describing a time when your workload was particularly heavy and how you handled it is a great view into how you approach day-to-day problems.

They want to know that you can handle your workload changing. Can you adapt? Basically, they want you to show them the tools or the process you'd use to handle that situation. So, you walk them through it.

You should say something like, "We all have times when our workloads become heavier than they normally are. I've found that the best thing to do is to take a look at what I have to do and prioritize tasks. What I've found is that not everything has to be done immediately. Some things are more mission-critical than others, and in times of stress you have to be able to prioritize."

And then you tell a short story that reflects your experience in prioritizing tasks in high-stress situations. (Use the STAR technique.)

Or you'd say something like, "In those situations, I take a look at what the workload is and prioritize critical tasks. I speak with my supervisor to see if there's a need for help in prioritizing from his point of view and execute. Just taking that look at it helps me feel less stressed and more in control."

And then you can tell a story about providing assistance to your boss on a critical task.

Either one of those is a much better answer than, "I stayed until the work was done." Many people give an answer that focuses on the long hours they worked on a project because they want that employer to know they work hard, but I think it's even more important for that employer to know that you can work smart.

I'm not saying don't talk about getting things done. Of course, talk about your follow-through and your dedication. But take them through your **thought process of how you approach a problem and think critically about it** and make great decisions that will benefit the company. It will make you stand out from other candidates and be very impressive to your future boss.

Job Interview Question 5

Describe how you would handle a situation if you were required to finish multiple tasks by the end of the day, and there was no conceivable way that you could finish them.

Job interviews are like very intense speed dating—they need to get to know you well in a very short time. For many companies, talking about your resume and what you've done is just not enough. They need to know how you'll behave on the job, how you'll react to situations. To get to the meat of those issues, they use behavioral interviewing. You must know how to answer behavioral interview questions before you go into your next job interview.

This question, asking you to describe how you'd handle a "too much to do and not enough time to do it" situation on the job is a classic. Who HASN'T had to deal with a day like that on the job?

You don't have to get into specifics here… what they want to know is how you THINK. How do you approach problems? What tools or strategies do you use to approach and solve challenges in your daily life on the job?

With this question, it all comes down to prioritization: How do you prioritize tasks? CAN you prioritize tasks? They don't want someone who's going to collapse into a "get me to therapy" heap or explode in anger over the issue. And they'll know by your answer.

A bad answer would sound like, "I expect my boss to give me a reasonable workload and recognize that not everything can get done."

Another bad answer is "I would just until I completed everything, as late as that needed to be." On the surface that sounds good, but in reality, it says nothing about your ability to think on your feet, analyze the situation, and implement a reasonable solution. **That's** what they want to know.

So walk them through your thought process when you prioritize: Does everything truly have to be done today? Even though you may have 25 tasks, maybe the truth is that the person who wants those done can't really do anything with all of them immediately anyway. Maybe they can only deal with 5 or 10 of them in the next couple of days, so those are the ones you concentrate on first.

Or maybe in your position, you would have people that you could delegate work to. When you talk about how you'd do that, they get a peek into your management style, too.

A lot of people take on tasks and never really take a look at "When does this have to be done?" They just look at the list and pull it onto their plate. That's not strategic thinking.

Show them your strategic thinking abilities and you'll be very impressive in the interview.

Job Interview Question 6

Describe your work style.

Do you know what your work style is? This is a popular interview question, but a lot of people go wrong in their answers because they don't understand what that employer really wants to know. They're not interested in your personality or your likes and dislikes. (They're not interested in how you dress for work, either.) They want to know how you work.

So some people really shoot themselves in the foot because they say things like, "I'm really laid back." First, that's a personality trait. Second, no one wants to hear that. No one wants to pay for your moseying along through your day. They want to get their money's worth out of your salary.

It's not about your personal preferences, either. For instance, some people will say things like, "I'm not a fan of conflict." What's that got to do with your work style? Nothing. Work style has to do with the work.

First, you want your answer to mesh nicely with the job itself. How does your style fit with that job?

If it's a data-driven role, you don't want to talk about how you like to come up with creative solutions for problems. That's not needed so much in that job.

What they really want to know are things like: Do you like to work alone, or as part of a team? You may actually prefer one or the other, but you should know what the job requires. Most companies appreciate someone who can do both. Teamwork is important, but sometimes you've got to just saddle up and go it alone. Talk about how you are comfortable with both.

Are you comfortable with minimal direction, or do you need lots of details before you complete a task? I think it's important to be upfront with this one if you really can only function one way. If you hate being micromanaged and your future boss believes in it wholeheartedly, then you are not going to want that job and it won't be a highlight on your resume.

You always want to pick out a few of your best qualities (again, that fit especially well with the job you want) and talk about those:

- Are you organized?
- Do you work quickly?
- Are you a good multi-tasker?
- Do you enjoy taking on extra projects?
- Are you a great planner?
- Are you consistently a top performer?

You can't be all things, but you can successfully approach this question like you do all interview questions: with a strategic answer that thoughtfully addresses the question and provides an answer that meshes your best qualities with the needs of the job.

Job Interview Question 7

Describe yourself to me in one word.

Sometimes job interviewers try to get inside your head. Why? Hiring you feels like a gamble to them. The person who hires you has a big stake in you doing well on the job.

Remember the 4 basic questions of every interviewer:

- Do you understand the job?
- Can you do the job?
- Will you do the job?
- Do you pose a risk to their own continued employment if you don't do well? (This is a prime reason why 30-60-90-day plans are such great interview tools—they answer all those questions VERY well.)

The end result of all this is that they sometimes ask you weird interview questions like, "Describe yourself to me in one word."

This is a tough one. My personal answer would be "dynamic," because I change, I adapt, and I do whatever I need to do to succeed. That's a good, all-purpose word that could apply to many different jobs.

But don't think only about a word that describes you. That could lead you down the path to picking something like "happy" or "resilient" that might describe you very well but doesn't speak to the job at all.

As in all things in the job search and interview process, be **strategic**. Every part of the process is a step that needs to lead you to your ultimate goal—the job offer. Be mindful of that.

Think about answering this question not just by thinking about what you are, but by thinking about **what you are in relation to the job**...what the job requires, what would make someone a standout employee in this position, what you're going to do for them.

So "bright," might accurately describe you because you're smart, but "successful" might mean more to them. (If you're successful in other areas, you'll probably be successful for them.)

Responsible, motivated, dedicated, those are all good words. So are: strategic, flexible, creative, dependable, reliable, helpful, fair, honest, focused, steady, organized, enthusiastic, or maybe even valuable.

Bottom line: Think about the job itself and what a fantastic characteristic would be for someone in that role, and tell them the one that applies to you.

But here's an extra hint: They might not let it go with just your one-word explanation. The follow up might very well be "Really? Can you give me an example?" So have a story that tells about how you embodied that trait at least once in your work life.

Do you prefer working in a team or alone?

Even though asking if you prefer working independently or as part of a team is a standard job interview question, it's also a bit of a tricky one. I can't think of any job that doesn't at some point require both work styles. So even though you probably do prefer working one way or the other, you will shoot yourself in the foot if you say so. It's better if you are comfortable with both, and very important that you indicate that. But there are subtle distinctions in the wording you use that can make the difference between an adequate answer and a standout answer.

The standard answer that most people give: 'I work well either way—I'm great as part of a team, and I'm comfortable working alone" is an OK answer, but you can do better.

The way to be strategic about this question is to really know the typical working conditions of the job you're going for and how much of your time will be spent on a team or by yourself. That requires some research on your part—but that kind of job interview prep is an essential part of creating your 30-60-90-day plan, which you should be doing anyway.

If the majority of the time you'll be **working alone**, you can say, "I prefer to work alone, but I find that occasionally working with a team feels creative because we can bounce ideas off each other. I like to learn from other's experiences."

If the majority of the time you'll be **working on a team**, you can say, "I like the dynamics of working in a group, but appreciate sometimes having a part of the project that's my own personal responsibility."

The general idea is to say what you prefer without being negative about the thing you don't.

Maintaining a **positive attitude** is important, and it will make the hiring manager feel good about hiring you. Everyone wants to work with people who are flexible rather than rigid.

But here's **one neat trick:** Instead of just offering an answer, add a question to toss the conversational ball back to them. Say something like, "About how much time do you think will be spent working on my own vs. working with a team in this position?" Or, "Does the corporate culture encourage one style over another?"

Asking questions of your own like this during the course of the interview gains you more information while keeping the tone conversational and helpful.

Give me a specific example of a time when you had to conform to a policy with which you did not agree.

Even though a good STAR story is the backbone of answering Behavioral Interview questions, here's one where it's actually a good thing NOT to have a great story for. Asking you for an example of a time when you folded under pressure is a situational interview question that's even worse than "Describe a difficult situation and how you handled it." At least in that one you can come out looking like you've overcome something. In this one, there's not any way to make yourself look good.

Think about your choices with this question:

Did you not want to conform to the policy because it was unethical—but then you did? You may think of yourself as the martyr in that situation, but you'll just come across as someone who is OK with being unethical. That's not the image you want to project.

Did you not want to conform because you knew best? Saying that you knew more than your previous boss is a bad tactical error in an interview because then you're badmouthing them—and that's always a no-no. That answer sets you up as an adversary for your future boss even before she hires you—and she won't. Not with that attitude.

The truth is that the vast majority of directives, instructions, etc. at work you just won't be able to have any influence on. The few things that you can influence are still limited. You can try to communicate, grab more information, educate, and so on. But in the end, you're going to have to execute or you might lose your job.

But this question does get asked in interviews, so how do you answer it?

The interview wants to know how you would really react in a difficult situation. What's your communication style? Did you confront your boss? Did you avoid the whole discussion?

Your best answer probably sounds something like, "Sorry, I can't think of a time when that happened." If they press, you might give a general, hypothetical answer like, "I might ask questions or express concerns over a policy because I believe it's part of my job to support the team and that includes spotting potential issues before they become actual problems...but in the end the decision belongs to my supervisor and I always respect that."

With that answer, you've shown you're a critical thinker, a team player, and respect the chain of command. What potential boss wouldn't be comfortable with that?

http://careerconfidential.com

Give me an example of a time that you felt you went above and beyond the call of duty at work.

If you get asked to describe a time you went above and beyond the call of duty on the job, be thrilled because this is a great behavioral interview question that has the potential to make you look like an amazing candidate.

You should ALWAYS have one of these stories because it's a great thing to talk about how you not only met, but exceeded the expectations of your employer. That's value.

Before you go into the interview, think about what story you'd tell in this situation. Choose one that not only describes a past success but also speaks to your potential success on this job. Good choices would be ones that highlight skills you need on this job or tasks you'll need to accomplish, although stories that highlight good character traits are also helpful. Relate your story to the job you're trying to get in some way.

Your answer or your story should talk about a difficult situation that you overcame. Conflict and resolution always makes for a good story. Always tell it along the lines of "Here was the situation....we needed X done, these were the tasks that needed to be done, these were the actions I took, and these were the results."

That's the STAR method. STAR stands for the Situation or Task you faced, the Action you took, and the Results you received. It's just a process to follow to make sure you get all the necessary elements in your answer. I've also seen it called CAR: Circumstance, Action, Result. Same thing.

Do not be afraid to brag. This is your shot. In fact, this is also an excellent time to pop open your brag book and do a little show and tell. Show them the note you got from a customer or your supervisor that congratulated you on a job well done. Show them the graph of the stats that improved dramatically after you took action.

Brag books are excellent communication aids for job interviews. They're visual, which gives you another interesting element in the interview. Not everyone takes the time to put them together and bring them, so they'll help you stand out. And they provide powerful evidence that backs up your story: I can do what I say I can do, and here's proof."

Combine a great story with the brag book, and you've got a solid point in your favor in the interview.

Job Interview Question 11

Have you ever been on a team where someone was not pulling their own weight? How did you handle it?

Asking about any difficulties with team projects in the past is a great behavioral interview question, and interviewers love to ask it. Everybody's been on a team where someone didn't pull their own weight. Remember group projects in school? And at some point in this job you're applying for, you'll almost certainly be asked to participate in another one. So it's a fair question to ask.

Be very careful about what you say in responding to this question or you'll sound whiny. It never worked to whine to your teacher, and it's not going to work to whine to your interviewer, either.

When you face this situation at work (or in school), your best bet is to focus on what YOU are supposed to be working on, not what someone else isn't working on. Try to do your job as best you can and support the supervisor in getting the whole job done. Maybe once you get your job done you could help the slacker, but that's a case-by-case decision.

Hopefully, you can truthfully say that you did just that: "I concentrated on getting my own work done and then went to ask my supervisor what I could do to help him finish the task."

You never want to say, "I reported that person to my supervisor" or "I told that person they better step up and get with the rest of the team." Neither is a great response.

It might be OK to say, "I got my task done and saw that person struggling, and I knew that the team success depended on all of us cooperating and succeeding, so I offered my assistance. John was grateful to get some help, and we've had a great relationship ever since, working together on several projects."

Of course, that's a very general response. It might be more appropriate for you to be more specific in your story, or it might not.

The bigger thing I want you to see is that you never ever badmouth your former supervisor or your former co-worker. That always makes you look unprofessional. And it gives them the (generally accurate) idea that if you'll say things like that about those people, you'll say things about them, too when you leave. None of those things are going to earn you points with the interviewer.

Try to always keep your responses positive and focused on how you got the job done. That's great job interview strategy.

Have you ever had difficulty working with a supervisor or manager?

When your interviewer asks, "Have you ever had difficulty working with a supervisor or manager?" they're not really asking about your past supervisors. They're asking about **you.** They want to know how YOU are to work with. The answer you choose will tell them more about you than about your previous boss.

So if you launch into a story about how your old boss yelled at everyone or was unreasonable in his or her demands or was a bad manager, the only message they'll get is that you badmouth people.

If you talk about how your boss accused you of not working hard enough when you clearly did, they'll assume that you are someone who doesn't work hard.

If you mention a boss who played favorites, they'll think you're a difficult person to work with.

So be very careful about answering this question. Even if you had legitimate complaints about your old boss (and lots of bosses earn every one of those complaints), you can't say so. It's never a good idea to badmouth your former boss, for any reason.

If possible, avoid it: "I can't say that I've ever had much trouble working with anyone. I actually appreciate the personality differences I've seen in my various supervisors and found that I could learn something from working with each of those styles. It hasn't been hard for me to adapt to working with anyone."

If you can't avoid it, tell them the story along with your thought process. But keep in mind that any story you tell should be the Disney version: positive, and with a happy ending. For example, you could say something like, "I did get off to a bad start with my manager in my very first job because we had different expectations and at the time, I didn't know enough to ask about those before I started work. But I got some very good advice to go talk with him about it, and we cleared the air. It turned out to be a great experience for me, and it was a good lesson to take forward in my career. Good communication is essential to a productive working relationship."

See? You haven't said anything negative about yourself or about your manager. It was the situation that was difficult. You took proactive steps to resolve it in a mature fashion, and the end result was a productive relationship. (By the way, that's a STAR structure: Situation or Task, Action, and Result. It's a great way to tell a story.

Keep your answer positive, show them how you think, and add one more point to the plus column for hiring you.

How can you apply your specific skills to help the organization achieve sustainable growth and generate revenue?

To answer this question, it's very important that you understand the role you're applying to fill.

If they ask you in the interview how you can apply your skills in "X, Y, and Z" to help the organization achieve growth and generate revenue, you're probably interviewing for a higher-level position. At that level, you should be very clear and very specific on how you can help. What benefits do you bring to the table? Why should they hire you over someone else? If you can name 3-4 ways in which you would benefit the company in achieving those twin goals of growth and revenue, you're in good shape.

That means that you better have expended considerable effort to think about the company and the position before your interview. And you've moved into bonus territory if you've put that into a 30-60-90-day plan to show them how you plan to get started achieving success for them. There are lots of reasons why 30/60/90-day plans help you stand out, and this is a big one.

But the truth is, this question about growth and revenue is important to answer for every position. Every position has financial value for the company, or it wouldn't exist. There's really only one purpose or mission for every job, and that's to make the company money—either directly or as a supportive role. Every role contributes to the bottom line.

Even the janitor does his part by keeping the place spic-and-span so that customers enjoy and feel comfortable in that space (increasing revenue) and so that workplace accidents are kept to a minimum (reducing costs).

A waitress does not just serve food. She's the face of the company that owns the restaurant. She directly affects the customer's image and opinion of the business, and whether or not they come back.

I was once asked by someone trying to stump me, "What about the person who puts the screws into the plane?" To them, that person was the lowest on the totem pole. In reality, that person is crucial to the success of the business. No one wants a plane falling apart in the sky, do they? That would definitely be bad for business.

So what does the role you're applying for do for that business? How will your skills contribute to the growth of the business and generate more revenue?

If you understand how your job fits into the bigger picture goals and can show the interviewer how your skills contribute to those goals, you're going to do very well.

Job Interview Question 14

How did you deal with the situation the last time your boss chastised you or strongly disagreed with a statement, a plan or a decision you made?

There are a lot of potential landmines lurking in this behavioral interview question.

Maybe your knee-jerk reaction would be to say, "Why, I don't recall that ever happening and I can't imagine that it would." Why is that? Are you a yes-man? That's not a good thing. It could say that you can't contribute in a way that means anything.

Maybe it did happen and you're still angry about it because it was unfair and your boss obviously missed his medication that day. Be careful what you say or you'll end up badmouthing your ex-boss...a big interview no-no.

Maybe it happened and you're not upset because it happens all the time. To you, you're a strong, independent go-getter. To them, you're a loose cannon who can't be trusted to make decisions. So what do you do?

First of all, if that ever happens to you at work, you want to make sure that whatever they're chastising you about or disagreeing with you over isn't a simple communication issue.

A lot of times, that's all it is...a communication issue.

Then you want to seek to understand their position. What's their point of view? How are they coming at this and why? Is there something you could have done differently? If so, own it: "I should have done this differently." And in the future, you won't make that mistake again. Seek to understand, see it from the other person's perspective and 'fess up when you make a mistake.

If your answer is in fact, "I don't really have a good example of a time that my boss strongly disagreed with something I did," say so. Maybe you haven't worked that long, or in more than one or two jobs. But that answer doesn't tell them much about you, and they do want to know how you handle conflict. So follow up that answer with a bit of your philosophy on communication: "I try to keep the lines of communication open so that doesn't happen. But misunderstandings happen, so I would try to see if that was the case first. If I make a mistake, I correct it and take steps to not make the same mistake twice." Or whatever. Now they know that you have a reasonable response to difficult situations.

If you did have a conflict, don't lie and say you didn't. Very few people can lie without triggering a "hmm..." response in the other person's brain. They might not even know why they don't trust you, they'll only know that they don't.

Address the past conflict by walking them through your process: you hit it head on. You spoke directly to your boss about the issue, tried to see where he was coming from, and learned X lesson. Keep the end result positive. And if you do tell a story about making a mistake, make sure it's clearly a one-time mistake.

"I realized I'd made a mistake because I didn't have all the information. Now I ask a lot more questions before I start a project to make sure that doesn't happen again. I'm a much better communicator now."

Job Interview Question 15

How do I know you still have the 'fire in the belly' to do this job?

If you're of a 'certain age' in the job search, you already know that age is a big issue. It's a very real obstacle to getting a job. Older workers have a reputation of not being up on the latest technology, not being willing to adapt, not being willing to take orders from younger bosses, and not having the energy or motivation to keep up with a heavy work schedule. That's what this 'fire in the belly' question is really asking: Are you still motivated to work hard?

There are several ways you can answer it.

(1) You can say, "I understand that hiring is risky, but one of the ways I can help make you feel better about hiring me and knowing that I am going to come in and do what I say I will do is to have you talk to my references. They'll tell you that I am what I say I am and I am someone who will exceed your expectations."

I personally really like this response. Your references are always going to be strong evidence for you and I would use them to bolster my candidacy. Everyone likes a recommendation. Choose the best references you can (past supervisors, if possible) and prep your references before the interview and before they're called. (All that means is to give them a heads up that a call is coming and tell them what's going to be the most helpful to talk about.)

(2) You can lean on your past experience. "You know, it's only been 6 months since I won X award for performance." Or, "...since I accomplished Z for my company."

Your brag book would be helpful here, if you've got recent accomplishments to point to.

(3) You can turn it around on them. If that person is the same age as you or older, you can say, "Well, have you lost the fire in your belly? Because I haven't."

This might seem flip at first, but anytime you can point out a way that you're similar to them, that's a good thing.

(4) You can be straightforward and say, "I absolutely do. It's a new challenge for me that I can't wait to tackle. In fact, I've even put together this 30-60-90-day plan to show you how I intend to be successful as soon as possible. Can we go over it to make sure I've got the details right?"

I'm not sure there is a more definitive answer to the motivation question than a 30-60-90-day plan. Just putting one together takes a lot of work and says very clearly that you care about getting this job and doing it well. Once you start discussing your plan, they will see very clearly that hiring you would be a very smart decision.

Job Interview Question 16

How do you deal with difficult customers?

Dealing with difficult customers is a fact of life for a TON of jobs: sales reps, customer service reps, retail store clerks, receptionists, restaurant wait staff, and hundreds of other service-industry jobs.

The people in those roles are in the front lines. They are the face of their respective companies, and have a tremendous impact on the company's image, which directly affects growth and revenue. Your answer should make it very clear that you understand how important your role is and take it very seriously.

You can absolutely tell a story about dealing with a particular difficult customer (what the situation was, how you handled it, what the results were) and if you happen to have a note from that customer or your supervisor in your brag book about your positive outcome from the situation, that's even better. There's nothing more powerful than evidence that you can do what you say you can do.

But overall, you need to make sure that your customer service philosophy is clear, so your answer should sound like this:

"I deal with difficult customers the same way I deal with easy customers. I want to make sure they have an exceptional experience with my company. I won't let a customer say bad things about us, or things that aren't accurate, but if we haven't met their expectations, I want to take responsibility for that and see if I can fix it. If I can't fix it, I still want to make the experience as positive as I can by doing something that would make up for the problem—maybe give them their money back, or provide some other benefit so that they exit that situation as happily as possible. I want to treat every customer as well as I'd treat my grandmother. "

Do you see what this answer does? It lets them know that you take personal responsibility for your customers and their experience with the company. The reputation of the company will not suffer under your watch, because you will do what you need to do to. They can trust you, they can depend on you. It's another selling point in your favor. And it's exponentially a stronger answer than: "I hand them off to my supervisor. "

Personal responsibility is a character trait in short supply these days, it seems. If your answer to this interview question highlights that quality in you, you will absolutely stand out from the crowd.

Want other ways to show the hiring manager what you'd be like on the job and convince them to hire you? Bring a 30-60-90-day plan to your interview.

How do you deal with stressful situations?

If I got asked about how I deal with stressful situations, the first thing that would pop into my head is, "You mean like this one?"

As if you didn't know, job interviews are very, very stressful. The way you calm your nerves is by recognizing that it's going to be stressful, preparing for the interview as much as possible, and taking a few deep relaxing breaths before you start.

But now is not the time to make that joke. My philosophy is 'never let them see you sweat.'

This 'stressful situations' question is a legitimate job interview question. Who doesn't have stress? Every job is going to have some time when you're going to feel overwhelmed and stressed out. They'd like to know that you'll react in a calm, rational fashion instead of erupting into a temper tantrum, screaming, hiding, or something else that would either alienate your co-workers or be otherwise unproductive. Stress management is a valuable skill.

'How do you deal with stressful situations' is a more generalized version of 'Tell me about a time you found yourself in a stressful situation and how you resolved it.' Both are behavioral interview questions. If you get the 'Tell me about a time..." version, you absolutely should have a story to tell. I always recommend using the STAR method (Situation or Task, Action, Result) to answer it—it keeps you from rambling off topic and makes sure you hit the most critical aspects of the story.

If you get the more generalized question about dealing with stressful situations, you have a little more leeway to talk about your overall approach to handling stress, but always keep in mind that you're talking about work. Keep it professional and always bring it back to an accomplishment:

"If a situation seems overwhelming, I mentally break it up into smaller steps, or doable goals, and just focus on reaching each one on the way to accomplishing the larger task. In fact, that's what I did with XYZ project. We had a major issue with X problem, but I broke it down into 'what needs to happen first,' and concentrated on one step at a time. I was able to see more solutions to the larger problem, and in fact, we got the entire project done in record time."

Or, "I find it best do concentrate on remaining calm, maybe taking a few deep breaths. When I run into a customer who's upset, it helps them to calm down if I'm calm and we can work together to resolve the situation."

Above all, choose an answer that shows that you can meet a stressful situation head-on in a productive, positive manner and let nothing stop you from accomplishing your goals.

Job Interview Question 18

How do you evaluate success?

I think the answer to this has to be related directly to your work. Don't wax philosophical about what success really is, or what a successful life is all about—you'll just knock yourself out of a job. They don't care that you'll consider yourself truly successful if you have great relationships, or if you are able to retire to the beach at 60, or anything else relating to your personal life.

Always remember your agenda in a job interview situation: to sell yourself for the job. That hiring manager is your customer, essentially, and you're the product. You need to know what that customer's problems and needs are (that's why you do your interview prep ahead of time and ask questions in the interview) and your entire conversation needs to be about how you (as the product) meet those needs better than any other product out there...and in some ways, exceed them. (It's like the 'bells and whistles' on a product. What are the extras that you bring to the table that make you unique or even more valuable to the company?)

For this situation, success is based on the goals you've set for yourself, the progress you make in achieving those goals, and how happy you make those who you work for with you. It's based on achieving objectives and satisfying the people who are paying you for work.

So a general answer might sound like: "I evaluate success based on meeting the goals set by my supervisors, how quickly I accomplish those goals, and the feedback I get based on my performance."

Or, "Success means finishing a project on time, under budget, and to the complete satisfaction of the 'customer' of that project." (This could be your supervisor, the person you built a house for / made a part for / created a marketing campaign for / organized a wedding for, etc.)

If you're in a management role, you might say, "I evaluate success based on meeting my professional goals while ensuring that everyone on my team is working both individually and together, smoothly and in peak form."

You can talk about customer satisfaction, increasing revenue, gaining more customers, improving accuracy, or any other business-growth or revenue related goal.

And you can certainly mention a few things, and then toss it back to the interviewer: "How is performance evaluated here?" Getting some details about how THEY evaluate success (their performance methods) will help you hone your answers for the rest of the conversation.

How do you handle stress and pressure on the job?

Hmmm....how DO you handle on-the-job pressure?

(a) I cry, yell, or complain.
(b) I hide in the bathroom.
(c) I love stress! It's so motivating!
(d) I don't get stressed.

Obviously, the right answer is (c) or (d)...either one works. Either you get some kind of adrenaline high off of the pressure and perform better, or you maintain a Zen-like calm and don't ever get stressed out.

And of course, everyone knows that those are the preferred answers to this particular question, so if you say one of them without really meaning it, you run the risk of sounding fake. (It's a little like saying "I'm such a perfectionist" in answer to the 'what's your greatest weakness' question.)

If you really can honestly say that deadlines motivate you to work harder, then go for it...especially if deadlines are a big part of your job. That's a great thing, and some people really do work well under pressure.

If you've learned to take a deep breath and focus on the task at hand, then talk about that. (Although that may apply only to surgeons and bomb squad personnel.)

What you can do to answer this in an honest, authentic way while still making them feel great about what you say is to talk about how you have learned to deal with the stress of the job.

Maybe when the job becomes extra stressful, you prioritize tasks so that it's manageable.

Maybe you can say that you've learned how to harness the energy from the pressure and make it work for you.

However you answer, follow it up with an example of how you've dealt with a stressful or pressure-filled situation in a previous jobs or other situation (certain volunteer experiences can be pressurized, too).

All jobs can, at one point or another, be stressful. Retailers get stressed out during the holiday season, accountants get buried during tax season, project managers run into people who aren't cooperating with their timelines, plans get sidetracked, customers get cranky, and shipments don't arrive on time.

Because stress is everywhere, you always want to have an answer to this question in your back pocket. You always want to answer the question positively, one way or another. Think about what desirable qualities are for top performers in your area and consider how you exemplify those qualities. And tell a quick story that provides evidence of what you say to hammer the point home. It's all part of your job interview strategy.

Job Interview Question 20

How do you rate yourself as a professional?

There are people who will tell you that your automatic response to rating yourself (on a scale of 1 to 10) should be "11". They say that anything less would be admitting a weakness. I don't agree. An over-the-top answer like that is bragging, which is a lot different than selling yourself for the job.

I think that if you answer "11," you're running a strong risk of coming off as arrogant in the interview, and I don't know too many hiring managers who relish the thought of hiring someone who thinks they're more than perfect. It makes for a strained working relationship.

I think that on a scale of 1 to 10 (10 being the highest), that an answer of 6, 7, or 8 is a reasonable, positive, sincere-sounding answer. It means that you recognize that you have room to grow and develop and become more and better than you are today.

If you're a young rookie, straight out of school or with only one job under your belt, you should answer 6 or 7.

If you're anything else, answer 7 or 8.

Only a true Subject Matter Expert with a lot of experience should put themselves at a 9 or a 10.

But once you give your answer (and pay attention to the surprise on their faces when you don't give the automatic, knee-jerk, follow-the-crowd response of '11'), offer an explanation of why you rate yourself that way.

Say, "On a scale of 1 to 10, I see 5 as a true average, and a 10 as perfect. I believe I'm better than average, and I don't know that anyone could be a 10, because no one's perfect."

Talk about how you rate yourself based on how others perform in the same roles that you have had.

In every arena, there are 4 or 5 (at least) things that set people apart...what are they in yours? How do you rate in each of those areas?

You really have to know yourself and your 'market' in order to answer this question. If you're in the job search, you better know these things anyway. You can't sell yourself for the job otherwise. And it makes it pretty hard to negotiate salary unless you know what you're worth.

If you can answer this question with a sincere, honest, reasoned response, you're going to stand out from the other candidates and earn big points with the interviewer.

Job Interview Question 21

How does this position fit in with the career path you envision for yourself?

I think a lot of people hurt themselves with their answer to this career question.

To be fair, it's hard to answer, just like "Where do you see yourself in 5 years?" or "What are your long-term goals?" Unless you're a person who has their life planned out, it's hard to predict what you'll want to be doing that far down the road. Especially if you're just starting out and still learning what jobs you love and what jobs you could do without.

But.

Employers like to see people who don't just float along with the tide. What's going to motivate you to do a great job for them (besides the paycheck)? What's going to make you want to do more, be better, take on new tasks, achieve? Do you have vision? Can you plan?

And, your answer tells the interviewer whether you want just any job or whether you're interested in THIS job.

That's a big part of what they're asking here: "Why THIS job?"

My general response to this question would concentrate on what I'm going to learn from this job:

"I would say that my career path is such that my career serves me, and I serve my career. I'm looking to grow and become more and contribute more and be more than I am today in my next role. And I know that if I do that I'll be rewarded professionally, personally, and financially. This position fits that for me because it's a growth role that will benefit me professionally because I'm going to be able to learn and develop more skills. As I do well, I'm going to be paid financially and personally in terms of personal satisfaction. It's a stepping stone to the next role. It's an opportunity to hone my skill set. It's an opportunity to learn this particular skill."

If you have a general end destination in mind, that's great. Talk about how this job is going to help you meet that goal. But only in the most general terms: "I plan to add value in this position, develop my skills to help grow the company, and eventually move into roles of greater responsibility." An answer along these lines tells them you're ambitious without any negative side effects, like being a threat to the interviewer's job.

Bottom line: You don't have to have a written-in-stone life plan done to answer this question. You just have to know what you're getting out of this job besides the paycheck.

Job Interview Question 22

How have you responded to a colleague who is putting you down at work?

This is a pretty specific question, but it's basically just another version of "How do you react in difficult situations?" This type of question is often asked in one version or another in behavioral interview situations. Employers want to get a sense of your judgment and decision-making abilities. Your answer here gives them a good idea of how you react to stress.

However, this really is a very specific question, and you have to answer it as it's asked. In this case, it's very possible that you just haven't had that happen. So if it's true, it's OK to say, "I'm glad to say that I haven't had that happen."

I've never had someone put me down. I've had someone criticize me to my boss, and he was in a larger role than me, so that was bad. But my boss saw his criticism as a weakness on his part because she saw that I was a threat to him. Even though she told me about the criticism and suggested ways I could be less threatening to him, I didn't do anything different except try not to step on his toes. I certainly didn't call him on the carpet. It wouldn't have been productive.

In some cases, maybe it would be productive to speak directly to that person and help them see how it's not only damaging to you, it's damaging to them (as it was to the person who criticized me).

You could also talk to your superior, but when you do that you're admitting that you can't handle a difficult situation on your own.

In some companies, people file complaints with Human Resources, but I don't think it's a good career move. Again, it's saying that you can't handle things on your own.

If you haven't had this happen, just say so and don't spend time talking about what you might do in that situation. You always have to think strategically in an interview situation, and wandering down paths of "what if" is not going to be a benefit to you.

If you have had this happen, it's important that you frame your answer in a positive fashion. Don't tell the story about how you went to HR. Don't tell the story about how you reported them to your boss. Don't talk about what a jerk that person was and how glad you are that in this job, you won't have to deal with them anymore. You don't ever want to concentrate on the negative in your interview answers, because it just reflects badly on you.

Tell a story that says, "I'm a capable professional with good judgment and the ability to handle difficult situations on my own and get to a positive outcome."

How long will it take for you to make a significant contribution?

I love, love, love this question. This is a 'roll out the red carpet, here's your golden ticket' opening to introducing your 30-60-90-day plan.

If you've never heard of a 30 60 90 day plan, it's very simple: it's a strategic plan for what actions you will take in your first 3 months on the job to ensure a successful transition from brand-new employee to fully-functioning, productive leader or member of the team. The first month usually requires some training, some getting to know the company's procedures and systems, and by the third month you should be at the point where you're initiating at least a few projects, sales, policies, improvements, etc. on your own. The more specific it is in the details to the company you're interviewing with, the better.

Why are these so great?

First, the research required to create a good plan automatically makes you a very well-prepared, knowledgeable candidate.

That's impressive. It's very obvious that you know what you're doing—even if you've never done that job before.

Second, they demonstrate all those character traits that hiring managers look for but that are very hard to pin down: enthusiasm, drive, initiative, personal responsibility, goal-setting, and much more.

Third, as you go through the plan with your future supervisor, he or she begins to visualize you in the job. Once they can "see" it, they're much more likely to offer you the job.

I've seen these plans get offers for people on the spot, I've seen them get offers for people that were for positions at higher levels than what they interviewed for in the first place, and I've seen them get offers for candidates who were less qualified than their competitors. If there ever were a job interview miracle tool, this would be it.

So...create your own 30/60/90-day plan for your next interview. I have tons of information about these plans on my blog at Career Confidential.

And when the interviewer says, "How long will it take for you to make a significant contribution?" you're not stuck with responding, "I don't know...6 months to a year?" or, "Well, I'd really have to get settled in to see, but I would hope to start making real progress soon."

Instead, you could say, "I'm so glad you asked. I've thought about that quite a bit, and I've put together a preliminary plan for what I could do to get rolling as fast as possible. Can I get your input on it?"

When they say "yes," you walk them through your very detailed plan for success and get their feedback. Even if you don't have all the details right, the conversation you'll have will, without a doubt, be the best interview you've ever had.

Job Interview Question 24

How long would you plan to stay with us?

Asking about your future plans in this way is really not asking you about your future plans. You don't have to go into your 5-year plan or your career goals. It's a brief question that requires only a brief answer.

Personally, my response to that question would be to smile and say, "How long would you like me to stay?" (But then, I often go for the humor.)

Another great response might sound something like this: "I plan to stay as long as I can. I don't want to change jobs if I can avoid it. I understand that there are learning curves to deal with, and that the grass isn't always greener and all that, but there's also something to be said for history and being able to rely on people."

For some people, this question is a beautiful thing. If you've worked somewhere for a long time, then you can say, "I stayed at my last job for 14 years. Do you think I'll be able to stay that long here?"

But if you have "short-gevity" rather than longevity, you might have to help them understand why you haven't stayed long at the other jobs, IF it puts you in a positive light.

Maybe there was a layoff situation or a reduction-in-force that was just a matter of "first in, first out" and had nothing to do with you or your performance. You can say that you would never have left that job.

Maybe you just outgrew your job. It was a small company, or there was just no place for you to go with your new skill set so you had to look outside the company. Everyone understands the desire to improve and grow and accomplish.

Either of those explanations is really something that's out of your control, so they don't reflect negatively on you.

But what if you don't have a nice convenient excuse? Maybe you have to do a little confessing: "I made a mistake. I left too soon and I will never make that mistake again. I understand now that just because the grass looks greener, doesn't mean that it is." It's OK to admit that you made a mistake and that you learned your lesson.

Hiring you is an investment for the company. They end up spending a lot of time and money in the hiring process, training you, getting you settled in. It takes time to get someone up to full-capacity. They'd rather you not work for a few months and then take off for greener pastures. Eliminate that doubt with your answer and call it good.

http://careerconfidential.com

Job Interview Question 25

How much money did / do you make?

Here's a question guaranteed to make you uncomfortable in the job interview process. It's one of the big hot-potato questions. No one wants to say a number first. But you don't have to feel pressured or stressed. There are some great ways to handle this question.

In general, for all salary issues that crop up before you have an offer in your hand, your first goal should be to deflect. Try to avoid talking about money for as long as you possibly can. (That's why you never, ever bring up money questions yourself.) You want them to fall in love with you before you start talking about commitment. Your bargaining position will be much stronger when they decide they want you to work for them. It will be easier to negotiate salary and ask for what you want.

If you can't deflect, there are a couple of ways you can go:

(1) You can go ahead and tell them how much you make because it's not relevant to this job.

(2) You can refuse to tell them how much you make because it's not relevant to this job.

In both cases, the reason it's not relevant is that it's probably a pretty good bet that this job has different (probably greater) responsibilities than your last one. So it's easy to make the case that what you made in your last job doesn't matter so much, because this job is different.

In my personal opinion, it's not a big deal to tell them how much you made in your last job. In my experience as a recruiter, most companies have a salary range for the position and they won't make an offer outside of that range. They're asking the question because they just want to make sure they can afford you.

This is where doing your homework will pay off for you, too. Your research will tell you what a reasonable pay range is for that position, in that part of the country. You can easily find out what they should be offering you for this job. If they do try to lowball you, you'll know it and can negotiate...after you have the offer in your hand.

If you feel strongly about not revealing what you make (and many people do), you can absolutely say, "My previous position doesn't really relate to this one, so I'm not comfortable discussing my past salary. But I really want to answer any questions about my skills or qualifications to see if we can agree that I'm the right person for the job, and I'm sure that if we do, we'll be able to come to an agreement on compensation, too. I'm really excited about the possibility of working here."

Or you could turn it around on them: "What is the salary range you're offering for this position? "When they tell you, say "I'm completely comfortable with that range. If I'm offered a salary within that range, I won't turn the offer down because of the money."

But please remember that every situation, every interview is different. A negotiation is a dance, not a step-by-step formula. You've got to take the temperature of your own situation and see what you think you can manage doing. But the more you research ahead of time, the better off you'll be.

http://careerconfidential.com

Job Interview Question 26

How was your working relationship with your previous supervisor?

How was your working relationship with your last boss? This is an attitude question for sure. They don't really care about your last boss, they care about **you**. Hiring managers know that past behavior predicts future performance, so they are very interested in your answer. Are you going to trash your old boss? Are you going to complain about how you were misunderstood? Or are you going to talk about how much you learned?

This is a pretty standard job interview question, so make sure you're ready for it.

Hopefully, this is an easy one because you got along great. Even if that's true, it's important that you elaborate a little bit on what you learned from that person that will help you succeed in this new job. The hiring manager doesn't want to only hear, "Great!"

Your being 'coachable' is a big deal to your future manager. They want someone who is willing to learn and who can take criticism and improve.

Even if you didn't get along so well with your last boss, it's important to try to keep this answer positive without lying about it. You should never out and out lie—first, it's just not a good thing and second, very few people can lie without setting off some signal you're lying in the hiring manager's subconscious mind.

Think about the positive things you learned from that relationship and talk about that. There's got to be something. Any kind of negativity from you in the interview only reflects badly on YOU. It makes you look like a whiner or complainer. But you can sort of turn lemons into lemonade.

If there was a real personality clash, you can say, "Our personalities were very different, so at times it was difficult for me, but it taught me a lot about how to adapt to another person's work style and made me a well-rounded person."

You might have to ponder that for a while to be able to come up with something positive if you worked for the Boss from Hell, but it's worth it. Being able to maintain a positive outlook and response even in the face of a difficult or stressful job situation is a huge plus for you.

And always remember that your focus is to sell yourself for this job, so try to bring it back around to how what you learned at that job from that boss will contribute to your success in this one.

If you do have a difficult situation you can't think of a way to talk about positively, consider hiring a career coach to help you.

How would you feel about working for someone who knows less than you?

It's not ideal to work for someone who does, in fact, know less than you. In fact, it's kind of aggravating. But typically, they don't know less than you in all areas. There is usually a reason they are where they are. They must know more than you in at least one little area, or they wouldn't be the person in charge. Right?

Even if you can't learn something from them (because for some reason they're The Anointed One), then help them be successful. Because if you help them be successful, typically they will help you be successful. But I digress...

The real crux of the issue this question tries to get at is this: Do you understand that there are people who know more than you and you can learn something from them?

There are some personality types this is a big issue for, but typically the folks who have a problem with this are older employees, the Over-50 crowd, who don't think they can learn anything from some young whippersnapper. If you're an older worker, you have to be aware of this stereotype and be careful of what you say in the interview. If you talk critically about the 'younger generation,' or tell a story about some 25-year-old idiot you worked with last, it will just reflect negatively on you. Even if he was an idiot.

This interview question is poking around for your sore spot. (It's similar to the 'how do you handle stressful situations' question.) They're looking for negativity. Are you going to be negative? I hope not.

In some jobs, you are going to go in and work for someone who's younger than you. For some people, that's no big deal and you can tell it's no big deal when you talk to them about it in the interview.

They say things like, "I usually find that even if someone knows less than me in one area, they know more than me in another one. I can learn something useful from just about everyone and I enjoy the process."

For others, who use that snarky tone and say things like "It can be aggravating, but I try to teach them what I know without being too threatening" or something similar that sounds positive but really isn't, what flashes through the interviewer's mind is, "My gosh, I'd hate to be the one managing this person because they are trouble." And your job offer disappears, just like that.

http://careerconfidential.com

Job Interview Question 28

How would you go about establishing your credibility quickly with the team?

The best way to go about establishing credibility with anybody in any situation is to ask really great questions and try to understand the situation before trying to do any kind of magic trick.

(Incidentally, this is another benefit of asking questions in the interview...you show what you know by what you ask. If you ask great questions, it helps establish your own credibility as a strong candidate.)

A lot of people think you should jump on the white horse and charge in immediately with a quick, decisive fix, and that's not what's necessary in most cases. You can do more harm than good that way, and make a lot of people angry in the process with your arrogance and inevitable mistakes. What's necessary is to ask the questions that reveal that you do understand the situation. Then you can make a stronger decision based on the evidence, rather than a knee-jerk reaction.

In other situations, the best way to establish credibility is just to buckle down and do your job as best you can as soon as possible. Actions speak louder than words.

For those reasons, this question is a FANTASTIC opening to show the interviewer your 30/60/90-day plan. You can say, "I think I can answer that question best with this: I put together an outline of what I hope to take action on and accomplish in my first 3 months on the job and I'd like to talk it over with you." And you bring out your plan and go over it with the hiring manager.

In case you're not familiar with this, a 30-60-90-day plan is a written outline of the primary actions you would take during your first 3 months on the job. You research the company and the job extensively to put one together, because the more specific the plan, the better off you are. The research helps make you the best-prepared, most knowledgeable candidate, and helps you create a better, more accurate plan. Your plan shows that you are very capable of doing the job, even if you have little to no experience. It shows that you're willing to go above and beyond, if necessary, and it shows that you're a strategic thinker, that you can analyze a situation and prioritize tasks.

Both the plan and the discussion of it that you have with the hiring manager show that would buckle down and execute on those things that would help you establish credibility and be a productive member or leader of the team.

Job Interview Question 29

I noticed that you are applying for a position that is not as senior as your past positions.

Why would you consider a job that is, in effect, a demotion for you?

This is a question you might get asked early on in the process, like in a phone interview. If you have a lot of experience, it's going to be obvious that you're overqualified. So the question is, 'Why would you take a job that's less than what you're qualified for?'

There can be a whole host of reasons you can cite...as long as you never, ever say anything that sounds like, "Because I've been out of work for so long that if I don't get a job soon, I'm going to lose my house." Even if it's true.

That's clearly one of the big things they're worried about when they ask you this question. They're worried that you just want A job, not THIS job, and that as soon as something better comes along, you're gone. Or they're worried that you'll be bored. The job won't be a good fit and you won't be happy...which means that eventually, you'll jump ship. And all the money they've invested in hiring and training you is gone, too.

They want to know that the job is going to be a good fit for you.

Even though taking a job that's considered a step backward in your career is considered to be a little unusual in our super-competitive society, there are plenty of reasons you might want to do it.

Maybe it's a shorter commute. Maybe you tried working in management but what you really enjoy is the hands-on work of your industry. Maybe you just really like this company or the product they make. Maybe there's some experience you can get in this job that you can't get anywhere else. Maybe the culture at this company is a better fit for you. Maybe there are growth opportunities at this company that you can't get at your old one (because that was a small company and this is a big one with lots of room to advance).

Since those reasons aren't readily apparent to others, you'll have to explain. Communicate to the hiring manager why this position at this company is a perfect fit for you.

And then point out that the fact that you're a little overqualified for this job is actually a bonus for them because they're getting someone with lots of experience. In this situation, you almost certainly have more experience than the other candidates and that's a big plus for them. It's another selling point for you, and you should help them to recognize it.

Job Interview Question 30

If we hire you, what will we know about you a year down the road?

Some candidates might wander off the path they should be on with this question (as many do with "Tell me about yourself") and start talking about how they'll know you like football, that you make a mean cheese dip, or that you never take sick days.

Stay on track and use this question just like you do all the other ones to sell yourself for the job. All your answers to interview questions should be strategically focused on getting you one step closer to the offer. Always be thinking: "How will this answer tell them something relevant about me and how I am perfect for this job?" "How will this answer make them want me more?" Strategically approaching the interview works.

This question helps you paint a brief picture of what life would look like with you in that role. If they can visualize it, you're one step closer to getting the job. It's just like thinking about how a couch will look in your living room or how a car will look in your driveway. The more you think about whatever that is fitting into your life, the easier it is to say 'yes' to the sale. In this case, it's the job offer. Incidentally, that's one of the reasons 30/60/90-day plans are so fantastic. They help that hiring manager 'see' you in the job.

I personally think that the very best answer to this interview question is:

"If you hire me, a year from now you'll know that everything I've said to you in this interview is true."

Want to elaborate a bit on that? Say:

"You'll know and understand why everyone in the past has enjoyed and appreciated my work and would like to have me work for them again." (References are an amazingly effective re-source for you and you should always make sure yours are pre-pared for a phone call about this opportunity.)

Or: "You'll know that I'm sincere when I say that I'm excited about learning more about this job and this company, and thriving and contributing and producing and wanting to do more and help you guys with [insert job responsibility here]."

Or (if you want something more specific): "You'll know that my skills in X, Y, and Z were a perfect fit for this position based on the results I got from _____ / the solution I came up with for _____."

This question is really just another version of "Why should we hire you?" You want them to know that you're going to meet, and even exceed their expectations of you.

Job Interview Question 31

If you could be any animal, which one would you be and why?

Some hiring managers really like these oddball interview questions. Some think it's going to reveal more about your character, and others just want to know what you really act like when you're under stress or just thrown a curve ball. Questions like these do reveal your thought process and offer you a chance to show off your creativity and inventiveness.

As in all job interview situations, your best bet is to be prepared for anything. Thinking long and hard about the qualities that are necessary to do a job well is actually an excellent exercise to go through before an interview, because it can help you focus your thoughts for how to answer all the interview questions you'll be asked. How does your personality, your background, your experience, or your skill set meet or exceed what this job requires?

For this particular question, it doesn't matter a lot what animal you choose, as long as you can tie it into qualities necessary to perform the job well. Although I would generally stay away from animals that have negative associations, like snakes, hyenas, rats, or chickens. Or spiders.

What are the personality traits that are desirable for someone who's going to fill this role?

Just smile and keep your answer simple and brief. Name the animal, and then explain why. Give one or two qualities that you see in that animal that also describe you.

I have a friend who says you should always try to be like an eagle, which is great if you're a CEO, but that's a bad animal to be if you need to be a team player.

A horse is really strong...able to function alone well or as part of a team.

Ants are hard workers, and the ultimate team player.

Monkeys are quick learners.

An elephant is strong, intelligent, loyal to the group, and unstoppable.

A dolphin is also intelligent, and actually considered one of the smartest animals.

Dogs are seen as Man's Best Friend, so might be good for someone in a support role. With a dog, you get loyalty and friendliness. Also protectiveness, but that's probably only required for bodyguards.

(Sorry, cat lovers. A cat's independence might appeal to you, but they have a bad reputation for not giving a darn about you as long as you're feeding it. That says, "I'm just here to collect my paycheck.")

A fun way to end this discussion is to say, "What animal did you choose when they asked you this question in your interview?"

Job Interview Question 32

If you could relive the last 10 years of your life, what would you do differently?

Hmmm….what would I do differently?

I wouldn't speed when I was going to get a ticket…

I wouldn't have invested money in those stocks…

I wouldn't have bought those shoes…

Maybe those kinds of things are what come to your mind when you're asked about what you would do differently, but when they ask you that question in a job interview, that's not quite what they mean.

This is another way to ask the 'weakness' question. They're looking for your flaws.

If there's an actual problem or issue in your work history that's obvious (or going to be obvious soon), this is an ideal time to address that situation.

Let's say you took a job and you got laid off…maybe that's why they're asking that question because they see that short-lived role on your resume and this is a way they ask about it without asking directly. You can say, "Well, I regret quitting X job to take Y one. It didn't turn out to be a great move for me. Even though I learned a lot from it and I can see the positives in what I learned from that situation, which would be one that I would change if I could turn back the clock. It wasn't the best decision...but it was the best decision I could have made with the information I had at the time. Hindsight is 20/20, isn't it?"

You can't hide all your issues, but you can frame them in a way that seems more positive. You can tell your story as you like. (As long as you don't lie...if they find out that you lied, you're done.)

If there's no problem and your career's been smooth sailing, then you can be a little more philosophical about this question.

You could try making a deflecting joke: "Gosh, that's a tough one. I know we need to talk about a lot of other things in this interview, so I'm not sure that we have time to go through ALL the things I would do differently..."

If you want to answer it more seriously, say something like:

"If I look at it from a personal perspective, certainly I think we all have moments that we would do differently. But overall, I'm pleased with the direction I've taken, the decisions I've made, and the things that have happened in my career and in my personal life."

That's a good, non-personal, neutral answer that should serve you just fine.

Job Interview Question 33

If you had to choose one, would you consider yourself a big-picture person or a detail-oriented person?

> For want of a nail
> the shoe was lost.
> For want of a shoe
> the horse was lost.
> For want of a horse
> the rider was lost.
> For want of a rider
> the battle was lost.
> For want of a battle
> the kingdom was lost.
> All for the want
> of a horseshoe nail.

This is a 'work style' type of question—but it's a complicated one. Employers really want both.

If you're a big-picture person, they'd like for you to also be able to handle the details. CEOs need to be able to consider the data when they make decisions for long-term plans.

If you're a detail-oriented person, they'd like for you to also be able to recognize the bigger picture and not get tunnel vision, because you need to be contributing toward the larger goal. Organizations need both styles in order to grow.

So the best answer really is, "I'm a _____, but I can also _____."

What you say first should absolutely depend on your job...accountants should be detail-oriented, and CEOs should be big-picture strategic types.

"I'm more of a detail-oriented person, but I can step back and look at the bigger picture, just like you step back and look at a map, to make sure that I'm on track for the larger goal."

"I'm definitely a big-picture person because I think strategically in terms of where the organization needs to be in order to be successful and profitable, but I can focus on whatever necessary details I need to inform those decisions."

And if you have a good story about a time when you used both skills in a successful project, now would be the time to tell it. "I was the group leader for X project, so I had to keep an eye out for what everyone was doing and make sure we were on track for our goal, and keep a checklist of all the details that needed to be taken care of in order to get there. We completed the project on time with excellent results." (And say what those results were.)

Big-picture jobs require strategy, creativity, the ability to see the forest and not get caught up in the individual trees. Generally, the higher up you are in an organization, the more you should be able to see the big picture. So if you're working your way up the ladder into upper management, you should be (or should be learning to be) a big-picture person. Other big picture jobs: consultants, entrepreneurs, writers, counselors.

Detail-oriented jobs are in much greater supply than big-picture jobs. There are always many more soldiers than generals. But as they say, the devil is in the details. You can lose the war for want of a nail. Many of the highest-paying jobs are incredibly detail-oriented, so it's a very valuable skill. Detail oriented jobs: engineers, scientists, mathematicians, surgeons, administrative assistants, researchers, and just about any kind of technology-based job.

If you were a tree, what kind of a tree would you be?

This is definitely a wacky question. Sometimes it's "What animal would you be?" or even "What fruit would you be?" You might think it is ridiculous, but you still have to play along, or you'll upset the interviewer.

They're asking because they want to see what you'll do if they throw you off stride by asking a question out of left field like this, or maybe they want an insight into your personality. This type of question checks your creativity, your ability to think on your feet, and just might reveal what you really think about yourself. (They hope.)

What they DON'T want to hear is, "I would be an apple tree because I like apples." That doesn't tell them anything useful, and it really doesn't have anything to do with the interview or the job.

To answer this question (or any kind of question where you have to choose 'what would you be?', think in a broad way about the qualities of whatever it is that you're going to pick and how you would explain your choice. What character or personality traits would be useful for someone in that role to have? Think in terms of the utilitarian productiveness of your choice as it relates to the job you're applying for. What does that job require? And then be careful of the nuances.

For instance, if you were answering the animal question: To you, a cat might seem independent, but one manager told me that to her, they seem lazy. An eagle is always a safe choice for someone who wants to be seen as a leader. Horses are strong, smart and useful. Just don't pick something like an earthworm or a vulture.

If you're answering the tree question, think about how fruit trees are productive, oak trees are strong and reliable, but cottonwood trees spread trash that everyone hates. I wouldn't choose a Weeping willow, because that just seems sad. Sugar maples are productive, too (syrup). Evergreen trees are steady. Palm trees are flexible.

A lot of people go for the oak tree: "I would be an oak tree, because I'm strong and dependable."

If you just can't stand the thought of choosing a tree, you could try saying something like, "I want to be the tree that would be most productive and useful to this organization. That's my goal."

Or maybe you want to research some trees before your next interview.

Is there anything I haven't told you about the company that you'd like to know?

Toward the end of the interview, hiring managers will ask some version of, "Do you have any questions for me?" Your answer is ALWAYS going to be "yes."

You always want to have a list of questions to ask in the interview. If you don't have any, it makes you look like you're not that interested in the role.

Here are some examples of great questions to ask:

Why is the position open?

Either the person before you failed so miserably at the role they were fired (in which case you want to know so you don't make the same mistakes), or they were so good at it they got promoted (in which case you want to know so you can see what worked and get a head start on being successful yourself). Or maybe the company is growing, so they've created this new role to deal with that. The answer you get will tell you a lot about what's going on.

When do you want to have it filled?

A few candidates will be afraid to ask this question, but don't be. It is not too bold. You're just getting information that will help you be professional in your follow up. After you send your thank you note, you need to know when you should be calling to check on the status of the job. You need a timeline so you're not left hanging, wondering what's going on. Hopefully, you're following several job leads and have lots of interviews scheduled. You don't want to turn something else down because you're waiting on this one.

How does this role fit in the whole of the company?

This is a great way to find out about advancement opportunities without coming right out and asking about them. And you can find out about what other departments you'll be working with. It might uncover some company culture or organizational issues you need to know before you start.

Where did the person who was in this role before go?

Were they promoted? Where were they promoted to? Is that the advancement track the company generally follows? Do they like to promote from within? All this is great information for you.

Were they fired? Why were they fired? Is there something they did or tried that should be a warning for you?

What is it you like about the company? (Alternative questions: What do you find most impressive about the company? Why do you like working here?)

The answer you get from this question should uncover a lot about the corporate culture, and whether this organization is a good fit for you. It might even uncover some perks that you wouldn't have discovered otherwise....like maybe there's an on-site gym or childcare, or maybe there are stock options you didn't know about that would have an effect on your salary negotiations later.

Job Interview Question 36

Situational Response Question:
An airplane landed in the parking lot.
What would you do?

Most situational interview questions are like behavioral questions. They have some direct relation to the job...like, "You're introducing a new policy to the group and facing opposition. How would you handle it?" Or, "How would you handle a situation in which a subordinate was not performing to expectations?"

Others seem like ridiculous, oddball questions that don't have any relevance to the job at all...but what they do for employers is give them a window into **how you think**. How do you approach a challenging situation? That's why they ask these kinds of questions.

You never know what they might ask, and there's really no way to prepare for them. I've seen some crazy questions like:

- How would you move Mount Fuji?
- How many light bulbs are in this building?
- What are 5 uncommon uses of a brick, not including building, layering, or a paper-weight?

- Suppose you had eight identical balls. One of them is slightly heavier and you are given a balance scale.
- What's the fewest number of times you have to use the scale to find the heavier ball?

If you get asked one of these, just take a deep breath and roll with it. The trick is to walk them through your thought process. Talk your way through it, showing how you would approach, think about, or strategize about whatever situation they throw at you.

So if I were asked what I would do if an airplane landed in the parking lot, I would say something like:

"I'm not sure I would do anything. If there are a lot of other people around and they look like they know what they're doing, I think I would stay back and let them handle it. If no one's hurt, I don't see that I have to get involved in that at all, except for maybe calling 911. If someone's hurt, or there's the possibility that someone will be hurt, then I would have to execute something very quickly. But what that would be exactly depends on a lot of things: How big is the plane? Where is it? What do I have access to? There would be a lot of questions that would have to be answered before I decided which action would be the most effective to take."

What I'm doing with this answer is demonstrating that I could evaluate, analyze, and sum up a situation before I decided on which action to take. Immediate, 'charge in on a white horse' action is not always the best move. Sometimes it's more important to stop and create a strategy first.

There's no really wrong answer to these questions. Just take them through your thought process and reason it out. It will be OK.

Job Interview Question 37

Tell me about a time when you disagreed with your boss about a way that something should be done. How did you handle that?

You can't get away with saying, "That's never happened. I've never disagreed with my boss." Everybody, at some point, has disagreed with a decision the boss made about something. The question-behind-the-question is, how did you handle it? In this case, they're looking to see that you have good communication skills and an understanding of authority. Can you get a competing idea communicated effectively and respectfully (without being rude or obnoxious)? Can you handle conflict in a professional manner?

You can tell your boss that you disagree about the way something should be, if at the same time you offer suggestions about how something should be handled. I personally think that's always the best way: when you disagree, offer an alternative solution. Don't just complain. But if the boss responds by saying, "I appreciate that, but we're going to go in this direction," then if you want to still continue to be employed, you're going to have to give up. They're the boss. (Unless for some reason, it's incredibly un-ethical...but in most cases it comes down to a simple matter of 'what the boss says, goes.')

The story you tell should be an example of how you handle such a situation respectfully, professionally, and with good communication skills (just like if your boss disagrees with you). This is a behavioral interview question, so use the STAR structure (Situation or Task, Action you took, Results you got) to tell your story. Just make sure that it's a story that shines a nice light on you when you're finished telling it. You don't want to tell the story about the time when you disagreed but your boss was being a jerk and you just gave in to keep the peace. And you don't want to tell the one where you realized you were wrong. Tell the one where your actions made a positive difference on the outcome of the situation--whether it was a work-related outcome or a more effective and productive working relationship.

Here is a very general example:

"We were working on a big project for X, and my boss decided that we should take Y action. But I could see where that decision would cause us trouble down the road with A, B, and C. So I went to her, told her my concerns, and offered some alternative ideas [state what those were]. She saw my point and liked that I was thinking outside the box. We implemented my idea and it gave us X results."

Tell me about a time when you faced a difficult situation with a co-worker.

"Works well with others" is a major skill we're judged on from kindergarten right on into the workplace. (If only we didn't get so many 'opportunities' to hone that particular skill!) That's why you get job interview questions about difficulties working with supervisors, difficulties working on team projects, and how you deal with stressful situations. They're all trying to see if you can get along and be professional (and productive). It's a behavioral question that pokes around in your past to help them predict how you'll behave in the future before they invite you into their environment.

With this question in particular, they're looking for how you deal with problems and confrontations in general and how you come up with solutions. How do you approach a difficult situation? Do you have good communication skills? Are you empathetic? Are you very emotional? Can you remain calm? Can you find a solution?

You should be quick to point out that, "Hey, I try not to get into difficult situations with co-workers." Being able to consistently keep the peace is a great skill.

But you're going to have to tell them something. You can choose to talk about a communication issue you worked through, or a professional challenge you overcame with your initiative, resilience and problem-solving skills.

A communication issue answer might sound like this: "Obviously, there are personalities that I don't do as well with as others. Once when that happened, I just reminded myself that there's a reason they're in that company, that they're a valuable member of the team and I've got to figure out a way to work with them. We had problems because we failed to communicate, which hurt us both. I figured that I must be causing 50% of that problem, so I thought about what I could do to alleviate the situation. So I came up with X, Y, Z solutions that I could use to address this issue, made sure I wasn't coming at it from a position of negativity, and resolved the problem."

Keep your answer emotion-free (don't vent any feelings here), with a happy ending. They just want to see your thought process. They want to see that you can be empathetic and that you are willing and able to negotiate a situation in a peaceful manner with a good outcome.

Job Interview Question 39

Tell me about a time when you failed.

The key to answering the failure question is that you can't say you've never failed. I know you probably want to, because you don't want to be seen in a bad light. But you can't. And it's OK.

Everybody fails. If you've never failed, it means you've never taken a risk (which means you probably haven't made much progress, either) or you've never made a big mistake (which is impossible).

I've failed lots of times in my career. What's important is that I learn from my failures and I don't make the same mistakes again. And that's what's important for you, too.

This is not like the weakness question. A weakness is a flaw in yourself that could affect your work in the future. A failure is a temporary event that doesn't have to happen again, if you are humble enough to learn a lesson from it.

So first, you have to choose a failure, and second, you have to be able to articulate something you've learned from the mistake so you can transform it into a turnaround story with a happy ending. Everybody loves comeback stories, right?

As in: "Once I failed by missing a deadline for a project, but I reacted to that by taking a course to learn my Outlook program in greater detail so that I could use it to keep myself organized and always on time. I've been much more productive since then, so I'm actually kind of glad that happened because I learned a lot from it and I am providing a greater benefit to my organization."

Or, you could say: "I am naturally optimistic, which is a great thing for my attitude and my ability to work with people, but once it caused me to overlook a possibility for a problem with my project that turned into an actual problem. I learned from that that I can be optimistic, but I should always have a contingency plan in place. And I do. And actually, it allows me even more peace of mind because I know that I've always got a Plan B, just in case."

Do you see? You admit the failure, tell what you learned from it and what action you took to correct it or avoid it going forward, and show why it has made improvements in you and your work. And always bring it back to your selling points so you can continue to be strategic in your interview answers.

Someone who's not afraid to admit they made a mistake and is obviously interested in improving themselves and their performance is always going to be attractive to an employer.

Job Interview Question 40

Tell me about a time when you had to give someone difficult feedback.
How did you handle it?

If you're interviewing for a management-level job, you will almost certainly be asked this question at some point. Nobody likes to give negative feedback, but if you supervise anyone, it's a necessary evil. Managers have to deliver both positive and negative feedback on almost a daily basis, depending on the size of the company and the group who reports to them.

Since delivering even the most constructive criticism can sometimes be a sensitive matter, it requires some higher-level communication skills to do it well. Your future employer will want to know that you have those communication skills so that you can correct undesirable behavior or actions and still run a smooth ship.

They also want to know that you understand the nuances of this situation: how others might take whatever feedback you're giving them. You have to think about how they might perceive what you're saying, what the impact will be on them, what out-come you want, and what you might need to say to preface what you're telling them in order to get that outcome.

They understand, and I hope you do too, that delivering nega-tive feedback well is about being a little more aware than just de-livering information. It's thinking about how they will react. Will they receive this information well? It's about what you want them to do with the information once they have it, what you want the long-term effect to be. How do you want them to move forward from here?

You always want to make sure that you ask questions that re-quire them to indicate their understanding of what you said so that you can clarify that you communicated what you wanted to communicate.

So what they're looking for in this question is that you under-stand that some situations require sensitivity, thinking it through, following up, and maybe even learning from not doing such a good job of giving that feedback.

Give them an example of a time you had to give someone negative feedback, but only as an illustration of your larger philo-sophical point of what it takes to deliver negative feedback well in order to get the change you're looking for. Show them that you approach it with forethought and sensitivity and with an eye to-ward communicating well in a positive manner—even though it's a negative subject.

http://careerconfidential.com

Job Interview Question 41

Tell me about yourself.

Some people think this is an icebreaker question because it's one of the first questions of the interview (and because in normal circumstances, it *is* an icebreaker question). So they answer it like they would in a social situation and say something along the lines of, "I've got 3 kids, I love to run marathons, I'm a Steelers fan"...whatever. That's a mistake. It's the wrong response because that's not what this question is about.

When they say, "Tell me about yourself," what they really want to know is "Tell me something that will matter to me as I consider you for this job."

This is a golden opportunity for you to set yourself in their minds as a great candidate. It's completely open-ended, so you can say anything you want. So think about the job, the job description, and all the research you did before the interview, and put yourself in that hiring manager's shoes: what is he or she going to be the most impressed by? What is going to get that person's attention and make them sit up and take notice of you for the rest of the interview?

You might start with your education—what's your degree? If you had an especially high GPA, you might mention it—but if you didn't, then don't. Just talk about your degree. If you did course-work that is different from your degree but pertains to this job, this is a good time to mention it.

And then go into your background. Just hit the highlights: promotions, awards, or key accomplishments. Not necessarily the things that you're most proud of—the things that this hiring manager for this job will be most impressed with.

This requires some strategic thinking on your part before you get there—but think of it like tailoring your resume. You tailor that to the job before you submit it, right? And you're going to tailor your answer to this question before you give it. Just think: What parts of my story would be on this hiring manager's list of reasons to hire me? That's what being strategic in the interview is all about.

You don't need to talk longer than a minute or so—just deliver a very targeted message that says to that hiring manager: "I am skilled, I have accomplished some great things, and I can bring that to work here for you."

Job Interview Question 42

Tell me your life story
(more of your personal history).

Hiring managers want to find out as much as they can about you in the interview. It's a bit of a risk-management thing. The more they know, the less likely they'll make a mistake by extending you a job offer. But even if they ask you to specifically reveal more of your personal history, it's still very important that you remember that your focus is not to make a new best friend here...it's to get a job.

For that reason, here's how you want to talk about your personal story in the interview:

Skim over the childhood portion, even though they've asked you for a personal history, because your childhood is probably not relevant for the work you're going to do at this company.

Say something like, "Well, I was born and raised here" or "I'm from X state," or whatever, and then briefly hit the highlights: I graduated high school, went to college, received XYZ degree, immediately was offered a position with ABC Company, and moved on to X Company after that.

But here's the part that trips up most people (I find this with my personal coaching clients all the time): They just want to spit out the history, versus "dressing it up" to sell it a little bit.

Many job seekers almost forget that they are SELLING themselves for the job, not just reciting a career history. Dressing up your answer to make you a more attractive candidate is very simple.

Instead of saying, "I spent 5 years in the military," you could say "I spent 5 years in the military, where I was in a leadership position over 150 soldiers and we executed XYZ."

Instead of saying, "I was the coach of the Whatever-Whatever's," you could say, "I was the coach of the Whatever-Whatever's and I coached them to an ABC championship."

Instead of saying, "I was a lifeguard in college," you could talk about how big the pool was, how many people swam there, what your responsibilities were and how you were rewarded for it.

If you were an account executive in a certain role, point out that you were immediately promoted to a higher position because you were one of the top 5 sales reps in the nation.

Don't just say what happened. **Elaborate** on the things that are important or impressive. Dress it up a bit into 'selling statements' that tell them more about you but also sell you for the job. Focus on making what you're saying a positive thing...something that actively contributes to getting you this job.

http://careerconfidential.com

Job Interview Question 43

Tell us about a failed project.

This is a more specific version of "Tell us about a time when you failed." This is a big behavioral interview question. Why do hiring managers want so badly to ask about your failures? It's because we've all failed at one time or another and how we deal with it and react to it says a lot about our character and our work ethic. It gives them another perspective on how you deal with stressful situations, too.

Failures are difficult. I've had a few of them myself.

Basically, how I feel about a failed project is this: a failed project is never a complete failure because you should have learned something from it that will make you smarter the next time around. As long as you don't disappoint your customers and your superiors, then having a failure is not necessarily a negative. In fact, failure can be good for us because it means that we're moving forward, we're trying. A few lumps and bumps on the way are part of the learning process.

I like Michael Jordan's quote: "I've failed over and over again in my life and that is why I succeed." Michael Jordan failed all over the place, but he's also one of the most successful, most accomplished athletes in the world.

We learn a lot from our failures, and that's what the interviewer wants to know that you know. Did you take responsibility? Did you take what you learned and apply it to being better than you were before?

Choose a failure that you learned something from that made you even better at what you do.

If it were me, I would choose a project that failed because of something like organization or time management rather than something that was a central skill I need for my job. And I would choose something that happened a long time ago. (Which gives me plenty of time to show that I didn't make that mistake again.)

Give them the background of the story (what was the project, what was going on). Tell them what the mistake was and why you made it. And then tell them what you learned and what steps you took to make sure that it never happened again. You failed, you learned, you improved.

I want everything in your interview to be as positive as you can make it, and that means your answer to the failure question, too.

Job Interview Question 44

Tell us about a time that you went against corporate directives.
Why? How did it turn out?

I once did a survey of job seekers as part of my mock interview program, asking them to give me actual questions they've been asked in job interviews, and this was one of the responses. I almost couldn't believe it. This is not a normal or typical interview question. To me, this is a little like saying, "Tell me about the last time you shoplifted."

I might have disagreed with my boss a time or two, but I never went against corporate directives, and I hope that you haven't, either. Usually, going against corporate directives means that you don't care that much about your job.

(Side note: Don't say that you might have disagreed with your boss but never gone against corporate directives, like I just said above. The natural follow up question to that is, "Oh, really? When?" They might think to ask about your disagreements with your boss, and they might not. But the general rule I would follow is: On negative questions, **don't volunteer more information** than what they're asking for.)

And don't assume they're asking you to describe your independent, maverick spirit, either. Maybe there are some companies where being a maverick is a plus, but I'm not sure that I know who they are. Google's corporate culture is famous for its unorthodox style, but I think that even they would have a problem with someone going directly against Google policies.

It would be a very, very special situation where taking that kind of action would cast you in a positive light with the company (former or prospective). Like maybe some kind of whistleblowing situation. Unless you've got some story about how you saved the company from ruin by going against your evil boss who was bent on destruction, I think I'd pass on answering this question.

I would turn this question (and any other question that seemed overly negative like this one) back to them and say, "I've never gone against corporate directives. Does that happen a lot here in this company? Is that an action that's valued here?"

Maybe you'll get a picture of corporate culture that will either make you think, "Finally...a place for an independent thinker like me!" or will send you running for the hills to get away from what is surely a chaotic environment.

Job Interview Question 45

There's no right or wrong answer, but if you could be anywhere in the world right now, where would you be?

Let's see….if I could be anywhere in the world, I'd be at Lake Tahoe, or lying on a beach with a fruity drink in my hand, or riding my horse through the mountains, or at the bank counting the millions of dollars I just won in the lottery…all those sound like great places to me.

This is not a typical job interview question. But it's really no more odd than "If you could be any animal, what would you be?" or "If you were a tree, what tree would you be?" Hiring managers ask those kinds of personality questions with dismaying frequency. So why do they ask them? It's because they're trying to get a better idea of who you are. They want insight into your personality and work and they think that maybe you'll let your guard down with this kind of question in a way you wouldn't with something like "What's your greatest weakness?" It's understandable. Their reputation is on the line every time they hire someone. If you're going to be on their team, you're a direct threat to their job if you don't do well. They have a lot at stake.

But you have a lot at stake, too.

Job interviews are hard to come by these days. If you get one, it's a golden opportunity that you HAVE to make the most of. That means that you need to be laser-focused on your goal, which is to get the job offer. To get the offer, you have to sell yourself as the best person for the job. How do you sell yourself for the job? By answering every single interview question (even weird interview questions like this one) in a positive, focused way that adds yet another layer of reasons to hire you.

If you follow that logic along, that means that the best answer to "If you could be anywhere in the world, where would you be?" is going to sound a lot like this one:

"Right where I'm at. For me, the next step in my life and my career is an opportunity like this. And sitting here with you is the best opportunity for me to make the move into this position. So I can't imagine that there is anywhere else I would prefer to be right now."

That's what I mean when I tell candidates to be strategic in the interview.

Because there IS a wrong answer to that interview question, no matter what they say. And the wrong answer is anything other than "Right here."

We are looking for someone with experience…or, you don't have enough experience—why should we hire you?

If you're a new graduate, or if you're switching careers, you might get asked this question, especially early on in the process, like in a phone interview. It is a challenge, but don't let it freak you out. They are at least somewhat interested in you, or they wouldn't have even bothered to talk to you. So keep that in mind and maintain your confidence. They are a little concerned, but all you have to do is to sort of help them along in their thinking on this issue.

You've got a couple of good options in this situation:

1. Turn the tables on them.

Remind them that at one point, they didn't have any experience either, and someone gave them a chance. Say something like, "Well, at some point, you didn't have any experience either, when you were first starting out. And obviously, you've been very successful. Would you hire you again?"

At this point, they'll be nodding their heads, remembering and agreeing with you—that's always a good thing! This is a very logical thing to bring up, and it gives you a little bit of a psychological edge in the process.

2. Don't ask about this person's experience (or lack of) directly. Ask about the people they've hired before.

Say, "Of your team, have you ever hired someone who didn't have specific experience in your industry?" They'll probably be nodding their heads with you, and then you can say, "I know there must have been a few times when that didn't work out, but there must also have been some times that it worked out really well."

They're going to say yes, and start telling you about someone who was especially successful even though they didn't have exactly the right education or background or experience. That's your opening. You say, "That's great. I can be that person for you, too. I can take those same skill sets and deliver those same kinds of results." (This is a great time to follow up by showing them your 30-60-90-day plan that spells out for them exactly how you're going to be successful.)

Both of those answers lead that hiring manager around to thinking outside the box a little bit. And you're gaining a psychological edge because you're drawing that connection for them between you and a successful outcome in those reminders of how it's worked out well before.

Keep your confidence, remember that you're a great candidate who learns quickly, and realize that everybody had to start somewhere.

http://careerconfidential.com

What are some of your greatest and/or proudest accomplishments?

This is a great job interview question, but a lot of people don't do it or themselves justice when they answer it.

One of the worst mistakes people make is that they will say that their greatest or proudest accomplishment is something that matters to them personally, like their kids. It doesn't matter if your kids are saints who never fight, spend their weekends feeding the poor, and have just won the Nobel Prize...that's still the wrong answer. Being proud of your kids is fantastic. We all love our kids. But that can't be the answer to this.

Good job interview strategy requires that everything you say must be focused on selling you for the job. That's why you're there.

Your answer to this needs to be something that directly relates to the job, like being awarded X prize for achievement after being in a position for only 18 months...or being recognized as the ABC....or figuring out a solution for a big hairy problem that the company had been struggling with for a long time. It MUST be work-related: awards, accomplishments, successes.

If you fail to say something work-related, you could easily lose out to a candidate who isn't necessarily a better candidate than you, but who does a better job of focusing themselves on the job at hand rather than on their personality or family.

It's also a mistake to say something work-related that isn't especially relevant for this job. For example, you don't want to tell a story about how you solved a technical problem if you're interviewing for a sales job. Even if it was the most complicated technical problem in the world requiring advanced knowledge and serious expertise, they won't care if what they really want to know is, "Can you make a sale?"

Prepare to answer this question before you get to the interview by thinking about your proudest at work and choosing one that would be especially impressive to this company, for this position. Or, come at it another way and read over the job description and then think about impressive things you've done that match up with at least one of those requirements.

When telling the story of your proudest accomplishment, be strategic and choose an example that directly relates to this job. (At the same time, choose another story to keep in your back pocket to help you answer the "What are your greatest strengths?" question.) In your story, provide details. Try to quantify those accomplishments as much as you can because numbers are impressive as hard evidence. Don't be afraid to brag. That's what this question is for.

http://careerconfidential.com

What are your advantages and disadvantages?

This question is another way to get at your greatest strengths and weaknesses as a candidate. But in this particular one, they'd like a list of the pros and cons of hiring you. Don't let it throw you. It is a beautiful thing to be the one in charge of putting together that list (if only during the interview). You can spin this story like a politician and turn it in your favor. Don't lie. Just focus on the positive.

The truth is that they're probably aware of your advantages and disadvantages already. They've read your resume. But this is a golden opportunity to influence their thinking by addressing any shortcomings in your experience or background while explaining why they don't matter that much.

Or look at it another way, and it's an opportunity to show them that your disadvantages or weaknesses aren't relevant or worth even thinking about because your advantages or strengths are so strong that they'd be crazy to pass you up.

Remember to sell yourself for this job. You're the "product" that's for sale. The hiring manager of that company is the customer, and your salary is the cost or the price they will pay for the product. Why are you going to be a great value for them?

Be strategic. Answer every question with an eye toward the job description and goals.

Of course, advantages are easy. It's the disadvantages that are going to trip you up. One strategy I like when talking about your disadvantages is using a strength that you could improve on. Another one is using a weakness that either doesn't matter for the job or that helps you with the job.

For instance, if I were asked this question, I'd say that my advantages were that I am intelligent, driven, quick-witted, high-energy, and able to communicate at all levels. Those were all great advantages for me when I was in sales, and also happen to be helpful to me as a career coach and business owner. I communicate very well with an enormous variety of people and can quickly evaluate and analyze what a job seeker's problems are and give them a solution, which saves them time and money.

I would say that my disadvantages are that I'm impatient, not detail-oriented, always want to be a leader. But all of these things are problems that either help me do my job well or don't cause me any problems in performance. See, my impatience is something that causes me a problem in my personal life (just ask my husband and kids) but that serves me very well in driving me to achieve quickly at work. When I say I'm not especially detail-oriented, I would also say "and that's why I take the extra steps of X, Y, and Z to address that issue so I don't miss anything." The leadership piece is another thing that sometimes causes me trouble in social situations but is a very desirable quality in my line of work.

You are in charge of how you present yourself as a candidate, and you can tell your own story in a way that shines the most flattering light on you and your candidacy.

http://careerconfidential.com

What are your hobbies?

Asking about your hobbies and interests seems like an odd interview question, but companies are asking more and more of those 'personality' type questions these days in an effort to make sure you're going to be a good cultural fit for the organization. And the indirectness of this question is also sort of a fishing expedition for them to see if you'll reveal things about yourself that you otherwise wouldn't.

It's not an innocuous question. They will read things into your answer, whether you intend for them to or not, and they will be influenced by what you say.

You've got a couple of strategic opportunities to take advantage of when answering this question. The first one is making a connection with the interviewer. This is a great place to build rapport. For that reason, stick with talking about hobbies that most people can identify with. (You can't build rapport if they can't identify with you.)

So first of all, whatever you do, don't make the mistake of talking about your crocheting or your ultimate fighting championship! Those both can have negative connotations for various audiences. Crocheting makes you seem 'older' and less culturally current, while ultimate fighting will make some hiring managers worry that you have a violent streak. For example, even though I personally like to shoot my pistol in target practice, there are a few people that would not sit well with, so I wouldn't mention that. Instead, I would choose to talk about another hobby, like riding horses.

The second opportunity is a chance to influence how they think of you as a candidate. This is a fantastic place to talk about hobbies that make you look either energetic or smart. Running is good. Hiking or walking are also positive activities. Traveling is always a good one. Reading is great, or any kind of continuing education piece. I always like to hear candidates talk about taking classes to learn something because I think that says something very positive about you, that you're willing to invest in yourself and that you're willing to learn and try new things.

Especially if you're an older candidate, this hobby question can be a strong way for you to communicate that you have a lot of energy or that you're interested in new technology or that you like to learn new things. All of those things go to alleviating any fears they have about your age.

Just remember that even something as small as a hobby can help you build the case for hiring you.

Job Interview Question 50

What are your least favorite things to do in your role as X?

This is a slightly different version of, "What did you dislike about your previous job?"

They're trying to find out more about you and how you think. If you're transferring roles in a lateral move, your answer will tell them about how you will perform in this new job. If you're making a move up the career ladder, there's not such a direct correlation, but it will still shed light on you, your performance, and even on how much you understand about this new role.

If you choose an answer that happens to be a central component of this job's responsibilities, you've just done yourself some serious damage. You've demonstrated that you haven't done your research, and you clearly don't understand the job.

Make sure you understand the role and choose a 'least favorite thing' that will be only a minor, insignificant component of your task list for this new job.

Another option is to try to choose an answer that anyone would choose. That's an easy way to build rapport and avoid making a mistake. For instance, a common answer to this question for those in management roles is "I hate firing people." No one likes to deliver that kind of bad news. But be sure to say that even though you dislike it, you do it when necessary.

Some answers that I might personally give are:

"I really dislike dealing with failings…even though I always say that failure can be helpful, I still don't enjoy it. I don't like dealing with employees who are failing, a project that's failing, or a situation that's failing. Because I hate it so much, I do everything I can to plan and avoid potential problems in the first place. But I understand that some things can't be avoided, and I do enjoy the feeling that I get when we're able to turn around a bad situation into something positive."

"I don't enjoy paperwork. I enjoy doing things that are going to have a positive impact on my results and performance, but I don't enjoy the monotonous details that are necessary to make that happen in some of those tasks. But I also understand that even if I don't like them, they have to be done. They fall under my job responsibilities. And I'm very driven to make that progress happen, whatever it takes."

As in answering all job interview questions, be strategic when answering this one. Think about the bigger picture of how you're selling yourself for the job and stay focused on the positive.

Both of these answers are honest, non-cookie-cutter answers that, even though they're answering a negative question, bring the conversation immediately back around to a positive statement about what I will bring to the job.

http://careerconfidential.com

What are your pet peeves?

Why would they ask about your pet peeves in a job interview?

They can actually find out quite a lot about you by what you choose to say when you answer this question:

- Do you get irritated easily? (How long is your list?)
- Will you be a good fit for their company culture? (If you hate being micromanaged and they're very focused on being 'involved' with employee projects, then chances are, you won't.)

I've seen some articles that say you should say that you don't have any pet peeves, but I don't agree with that. Everyone has things that irritate them more than other things. You can downplay your irritation (the interview is not the time to go into a Lewis Black-style rant, for sure), but if you say you don't have one, it just sounds false.

So tell them one. As in all your job interview answers, consider what you're going to say before you say it to make sure it works for you and not against you. Obviously, make sure your pet peeve isn't something you'd run into every day on the job—like, you can't stand team projects when the job is going to require that at least 30% of the time.

Your answer will say as much about you and your attitude as they will about what your actual pet peeve is. So if you say, "I hate blowhards who are all talk and no action. They're also the ones who usually don't pull their own weight on team projects. I hate that, too." That reveals you as someone with a temper, a negative attitude and a tendency to make assumptions about others.

For instance, I might say, "I don't like negative attitudes. It doesn't help anyone, even the person who's being negative. If there's a problem, they should focus on how to fix it." That says that I'm someone who's focused on solutions rather than problems.

Or I might say, "I don't like people who don't work hard at their jobs. I believe that if you've been hired to do something, you should put 100% of your talent and effort into it to be successful and fulfill that contract you've created with the employer." That's an incredibly positive answer that speaks to your work ethic.

A great answer will say something positive about you and add another reason to hire you.

Job Interview Question 52

What are your salary expectations?

Oh, the dreaded salary question! The good news is that it doesn't have to be a big problem for you if you know how to handle it. The primary strategy I teach my job seekers is, "Do your salary research so that you know what the going rate is for that job in your part of the country, and then deflect naming a number for as long as possible."

Still, there are different approaches to use depending on who asks you this question.

If HR asks, respond with a question: ask what their salary range is for this job. They'll have one. When they tell you, say, "I'm comfortable with that range. If I think this is the right job for me, and you think that I'm the right person for it, we can absolutely come to an agreement. "

If the hiring manager asks, things get a little stickier, but you still have options. It's not always true that "the one who says a number first loses," but you do want to try not to be first.

It's totally appropriate throw the ball back to them, just like you did with HR: "That's a great question. We haven't discussed what the salary and compensation plan for this position is. Can you fill me in on that?"

50% of hiring managers will go ahead and start telling you.

The other 50% really want to know how much you're going to cost. They'll say, "Well, it depends on the candidate. What are **your** requirements?"

So you say, "I am really looking for a challenge, to use my skills in X, Y, and Z. I'm sure that you'll pay a salary that's appropriate for the challenges of this job. What did the company have in mind for that?"

This answer will divert a few more people, but a stubborn manager will say something like, "It really does depend on the candidate. Do you have a range?"

If you can't push back any more, say, "I have to be honest. This is a new position for me. I'd really have to see the total package, the entire compensation plan with all the benefits. My last salary was in the $55,000 range, and this position seems to me to be a rung or two above that in responsibility and in my ability to impact the organization, so I would expect that the salary offer would reflect that."

Salary negotiations are tricky business. One of the best books on the planet on this subject is **Negotiating Your Salary: How to Make $1000 a Minute**, by Jack Chapman. It's a short, easy read and it will fill your brain with all kinds of tips and tactics you can use that work like a charm. Find it and read it.

Salary questions can be difficult, but I want you to remember that your responses really do demonstrate your strength and confidence as a candidate. Stay calm, cool, and confident, and you'll be fine.

Job Interview Question 53

What are your workplace values?

Asking about your workplace values is similar to asking "What is your work ethic?" Or, "What are your workplace ethics?" They want to know what kind of person you are. What matters to you?

It's really an easy question to answer because your answer should be what your values are. They should speak to your integrity, your character, and your work ethic. As long as you're saying something positive, that's a good thing. But always, keep it tied to your work...they don't care that you love baby seals and spotted owls as a part of your commitment to the environment, unless you're applying for a job with an environmental group.

You can say, "My work place values are the same as my home and personal values" because that shows integrity.

For me, my answer would be "I do what I say I'm going to do, I follow up on my commitments, and I think of others before I think of myself."

Other great answers might sound more like, "I always try to do the very best that I can, because my employer is paying for a service, and I supply that just like I would if I owned a business and that person was my customer. My customer deserves the best I can deliver."

Or, "I believe that everyone who works for a company is part of a team, and it's important for us all to support each other and step up to do what needs doing to get the job done. I try to lead by example in that way."

If you've done your research into the company to see what their corporate values are, you can talk about which of your own values align with theirs. Now, please note that I am NOT saying to lie and just tell them what they want to hear. A lie is always eventually found out, and won't serve you in the end, anyway. You need to know what that company's corporate values are, so you know if you'll be happy working for them or not. Their core values are going to have a major effect on your career. You don't want a toxic corporate environment to hijack your own values and make you miserable. Environment matters.

What you say about your values should give that hiring manager an indication of what kind of a person you are to work with, why he should trust you, why you're going to be a great hire, and anything else that's going to sell him on the idea he should offer you the job.

Job Interview Question 54

What did you earn at your last job?

For most candidates, "What was your salary?" is a very uncomfortable, Too Much Information-kind of a question. But all potential employers are going to ask at some point in the process, often very early on...sometimes as early as the initial application. So why do they ask? And how do you handle it?

If your recruiter or Human Resources asks, it's because they're trying to make sure you won't embarrass them by refusing an offer over money. If you make $60,000 a year and this job only pays $40,000, chances are you won't take it and they want to know that up front. They get yelled at if they get hiring managers involved with a candidate they can't afford.

If you manage to avoid it during the application process, the hiring manager will probably ask you in the interview. The reasoning is the same. They want to know, "Can we afford you?"

If you feel strongly about not revealing that information, you can try saying something like, "Can you help me understand what information you're really asking for here? I'm not very comfortable discussing my past salary because it doesn't really relate to this job. There are a lot of other factors involved than just straight numbers. I would love to answer questions about my skills and qualifications for this job. I think this is a great company, and I'm excited about the possibility of working here. I know that if we agree that I'm the best fit for the position, we'll be able to come to an agreement on salary."

Or you could avoid answering by asking a question: "What's the salary range for this position?" When they tell you, assure them that you're comfortable with that range and if they make you an offer, you won't refuse it over the money.

If you try to avoid answering, you may face opposition and may even lose the opportunity over it. But if you keep the opportunity and get the offer, then you're in a very strong negotiating position, which is a great place to be.

The whole process is a dance and the steps are not hard-and-fast moves. Take the temperature of your situation and see what you think you can manage doing.

In my personal opinion, it's not a big deal to tell them how much you made at your last job. Why? It's easy to research salary and find out what the going rate is for this job and know if what they're offering is in the ball park. And, it's easy to argue that what you made on your last job doesn't have any bearing to what you'll make at this one, because they're different jobs with different responsibilities. Usually this new job will have more responsibilities and a higher level of authority, so it only makes sense that you'd be paid more.

In my experience as a recruiter, most companies have a range budgeted and they won't make an offer outside of that range, even if what you made before was below it.

If they do try to lowball you, you have options. Now you're in the negotiation process. They want you, but you haven't come to an agreement on the price of doing business yet. I strongly encourage you to read Jack Chapman's book, **Negotiating Your Salary: How to Make $1000 a Minute**. It's the best book I've ever seen for gaining insight on this subject.

http://careerconfidential.com

Job Interview Question 55

What did you like or dislike about your previous jobs?

This sounds like a 'get-to-know-you' question, but don't get too comfortable. It's another way to get at your strengths and weaknesses, and you can trip yourself up. Always remember your primary focus is to sell yourself for this job. Be strategic.

Think about things that you especially liked about your past roles and that are related to this job. Think about anything that would support the case for hiring you. What factors or tasks from your past jobs will be crucial to your success in this role?

When you talk about what you disliked, try to choose something that won't be a factor in this new job. Don't unthinkingly tell them something you hated about your last job that is related to one of the main functions of this one. Easy things to choose might be the hours, the commute, the travel time, the limitations of a small company (if you're applying at a large one) or the anonymity of a large corporation (if you're applying at a small company). Try to stay away from things like complaints about your boss or co-workers. Try to be positive.

Obviously, what you disliked will be a negative for you, but you never want to be too negative in what you say when answering job interview questions because that negativity reflects on you. They won't remember the details about your answer, they'll just remember your bad attitude about it. It will influence how they think about you as a candidate.

Here's an answer I would give:

"What I liked about all my previous jobs is that they were all strong communication opportunities where when I worked hard, I was able to make things happen and I was able to be successful.

What I didn't like was when I wasn't able to be successful. Or where I perceived that I wasn't able to be as successful as I should be, or where I had to work through issues that shouldn't have been there. I can't stand bureaucracy, or having anyone stand in the way of the success of the team that I'm on."

That answer tells the interviewer very clearly that I am driven, and very focused on achievement and success. Those qualities were critical to the roles and duties I performed in sales and sales management. In that answer, I added another layer of "here's why you want me for the job." That's what you should try to do in your answer, too.

http://careerconfidential.com

Job Interview Question 56

What do people most often criticize about you?

Watch out for this job interview question. This is another way to ask, "What's your greatest weakness?" It is also a fishing expedition to see how well you take criticism. We all have to be open to criticism in order to grow and improve as professionals and as people. Being 'coachable' is a big plus in your favor in the eyes of your future manager or supervisor.

I don't think you can get away with saying, "People don't criticize me, and I can't think of anything." You can't go through life without stepping on toes once in a while, and we all have room for improvement.

You could try to deflect it with humor: "Well, my wife can't stand that I don't put the cap back on the toothpaste." But a serious interviewer is going to press you for a real answer.

When you answer "What do people criticize about you?" (Whether you try the humor angle or not), your big-picture strategy should be to tell them a criticism or weakness that doesn't affect your job performance and in fact, may even help it. Then show them that you can deal with criticism in general in a calm, professional manner.

For example, I have been (and am still, on a regular basis) criticized for being impatient. That's sometimes a problem in my personal life and in my relationships, but that's always been a big plus for my professional drive and success. I know I'm impatient, and I do work to rein that in when dealing with relationships, but I use it in my professional life to propel me further and faster than I would get without it.

Maybe you take things too seriously. You can say, "I've been told I take things too seriously. It's true that I tend to be a serious person. I do have a sense of humor, but I tend to be focus on getting the job done first and having fun later."

If you have a story about how you addressed a criticism and improved, that's even better: "I used to be infamous for being overly critical, which stemmed from my focus on delivering outstanding results. I want all the details to be fantastic. I still am focused on consistently delivering those results, but I have learned to be more tactful and to offer compliments and encouragement with my criticism so that others perceive it as coaching rather than criticizing and it's worked out very well."

What do you consider to be your most significant accomplishment?

This is a fantastic job interview question. It sets you up to shine a giant spotlight on yourself as the ideal candidate for this job.

Never, ever answer this question by talking about something you achieved or accomplished outside of work. No stories about your kids, or how you climbed Mount Everest. Always focus your answer on work-related accomplishments.

But don't just choose a work-related answer. Choose an answer relevant to the specific job you're applying for. If you saved the company from bankruptcy in your last job, but you can't find a way to relate the skills you used to accomplish that to the ones you need for this job, it won't do you any good. Go back through your brag book, your performance reviews, everything you've got to think about a story that would highlight your fit for this job.

This is a classic behavioral interview question that requires you to put your answer in the form of a story. Don't just answer it by talking about the end result of your effort, as in "I ranked #1 among sales reps for 5 years in a row" or "I saved my company $5 million dollars last year." That's fantastic, but if you limit your answer like that, you're missing out on some prime selling time here.

Tell the story. (Use the STAR method—Situation or Task, Action, Result.) Tell how you approached the problem or the goal or whatever it was, how you thought about it, and how you used the resources you had available to start reaching your goal or solving your problem. You can talk about what obstacles you came up against and how you overcame them.

If possible, use your brag book as supporting evidence. (If you're not familiar with these, brag books are simply a collection of "good job" documents: award letters, performance reviews, reference letters, complimentary emails, especially good examples of your work, performance stats that don't fit on your resume, etc.) If you got some award for that achievement, or even a nice email from your supervisor or a customer, show it to the interviewer when you tell what happened. It will make a powerful impression.

With a really good story, you can show your critical thinking skills, your creativity, your work ethic, your skill level—all kinds of things that help sell you for the job.

Job Interview Question 58

What do you expect from a supervisor?

Be careful when answering this job interview question. There's a line to walk. They're looking to see: (1) do you understand the general supervisor/employee relationship, (2) will your style match with your potential new boss, and (3) will you take this opportunity to badmouth your previous boss?

Don't be too specific, don't be negative, and never, ever badmouth your previous boss.

You probably don't know too much yet about your potential supervisor's management style. If you get too specific, you might step on some toes.

Be positive when you answer this question, and try very hard to keep it neutral and generic. Now is not the time to talk about those things that irritated you about your last boss, and say things like:

"I'd like a boss who doesn't yell at everyone."

"I expect that a supervisor would not play favorites."

"I expect a boss to trust that I'm a good employee who doesn't need to be micromanaged."

You're veering off into negativity with these bad answers, and revealing more about you and how (not well) than you are giving a good answer to the question.

What you want to do with this question is to play it safe and think of it like a "wish list" for an ideal. Don't make it a long list...nobody's perfect. Just name two or three noble qualities that your interviewer can imagine that he or she has (maybe they really do), such as good communication skills, a sense of humor, loyalty, fairness, knowledge, leadership skills, a willingness to teach you something. Those are all good traits.

For example, I would say: "I expect a supervisor to communicate clearly, to treat me fairly, and to give me opportunities to do as much as I can for the organization."

That answer also has the added benefit of pointing out my desire to contribute and achieve within that company.

Other good answers might sound like:

"A supervisor should have good leadership and communication skills and should be able to offer constructive criticism."

"I would expect a supervisor to keep the lines of communication open with me and offer feedback when I'm doing a good job and when I have room for improvement."

"I would expect a supervisor to be adaptable to different employee's work styles and communication styles, and be willing to help employees develop additional skills to be more successful."

http://careerconfidential.com

Job Interview Question 59

What do you know about this company?

This is a typical interview question. Hiring managers want to know if you've done your homework. Have you done any company research?

You would be surprised at how many candidates can't answer this question. Other candidates get a basic working knowledge of what the company does from reading through the corporate website and think that's enough. If you want to really stand out among the other candidates and have a great chance of getting the job, the corporate website is only your starting point of preparing for your interview.

If you really want to be a "Wow" candidate, you have to uncover as much as you possibly can about the company before you get to the interview. You can't use the excuse that "Well, if the first interview goes well, I'll look into it more deeply then. Why spend a lot of time on something that may not go anywhere?" That's a bit of a self-fulfilling prophecy. If you don't do your research, chances are that the first interview will be your last one because you'll appear to be uninterested in the job. That failed experience will reinforce your behavior for next time, and before you know it, you'll be through several first interviews with no second interview and no job offer.

So where should you go besides the corporate website?

Google – When has the company been in the news? Do they have any plans in the works? Are there any blog articles about it?

LinkedIn – Companies put different information here than they do on their corporate pages. Also look up past and present employees, if you can.

Facebook- Companies' Facebook pages have still a different focus and can give you another perspective.

Twitter – Sometimes, employee Tweets tell you a lot.

Competitors – Research the company's competitors to compare.

Ask people – Tap into your network or ask your recruiter for the inside scoop.

Use what you uncover to make yourself a list of information about the company. Then when they ask you, "What do you know about us?" you can talk about their products, services, reputation, place in the market, problems, mission, history, and more. You'll be better-equipped to talk about your skills in relation to their needs, and you'll have more-informed questions to ask in the interview, too.

Then you can say something like, "I know X, Y, and Z, and that's why I am very excited about working here. I think I'm an especially good fit for you because of A, B, and C." And you've just given them another reason to hire you.

What do you wish you'd done better?

When you are asked this question in job interview, please be aware that they are referring to your career, not your life. You could say that you wish you'd hired someone to tile your floor instead of doing it yourself, or that you wish you'd planned your vacation better, or you wish you'd studied more before your SATs, but those answers won't satisfy your interviewer. This is a tough job interview question.

What would you do differently in your career? What do you wish you'd done better? This question is a behavioral interview-style way to find out "what's your greatest weakness?" It's also closely-related to "What's your biggest failure?" Hiring managers know that we're onto that question the way it's normally asked, so they just ask it a different way. But with this question, you must have a story to tell.

Asking this question also is a way for them to find out about how you deal with adversity and difficult. They want to know that you are mature and that you can learn from your mistakes. It's a peek into your thought process. What they're hoping you'll be able to do is communicate a story or situation (what happened), say what you wish you'd done better, and then provide an example of when you did do it better. Because that's the ideal kind of employee—one who learns from their mistakes.

Even if you're telling them a real story about a real mistake, try to give them what they want to hear without choosing something that would directly affect your performance at this job. Nobody wants to hire an accountant who had organizational problems at her last job. Nobody wants to hire a sales rep who had an issue with a co-worker that you couldn't work out—because that shows an issue with interpersonal and communication, a fatal flaw for sales reps. So try to talk about a real mistake that you learned something significant from that would never affect your performance at this job.

For instance, that accountant might say, "It's always easier to look back to find room for improvement, isn't it? Once, I was having a disagreement with a co-worker on a project, so I went to my supervisor to try to figure out what I was doing wrong and get to a solution. My intentions were sincere, but the result was that it angered my co-worker because she thought I was trying to get her into trouble. I have learned since then that direct communication is always best, and I am very conscious about those co-worker relationships. It actually was a good experience because I am a much better communicator and team player now."

Now you're an accountant who's also got good communication skills and can be a team player. You've turned a negative into a positive. That's good job interview strategy.

Job Interview Question 61

What excites you and scares you about this position?

This is a tough question. I think it sounds like another version of "what are your greatest advantages and disadvantages?" or another way to ask about your strengths and weaknesses. They're looking to see if you'll tell them about any issues or problems you might have, while they're assessing your enthusiasm and approach to the job.

As with most interview questions, keep it as positive as you can. I don't normally have a fear when I go into a new job and I don't think that you should voice one, either.

Why not? Well, think about this interaction you're having with this hiring manager. This process you're going through to jobs a sales process. You're the product and he (or she) is the buyer. Why would they want to choose a product that wasn't certain it could do the job? Put yourself in the buyer's shoes: would you buy something at a store that "hoped" it could do what you needed it to do, as long as nothing went wrong? Of course not. You'd buy the product that said, "I can do X...no question. I've done it before and I can do it for you."

For those reasons, the best answer is something like, "Nothing scares me about this job, and everything about it is exciting because I know that I can impact A, B, and C. I know this because I've done it before." ("A, B, and C" are those outcomes the company wants to affect with the tasks of this role.)

If you haven't actually done this job before, you can say, "I've done something very similar before." And make sure you know why and how your skills that you learned in other places transfer to this one.

Another great answer sounds like this: "I can't say that I'm scared at all about this job. I'm excited about the opportunity to exceed your expectations, and I'm excited about what the future holds for me once I do that."

If you're really pressed for an answer to the scared portion of this question, say "The only things that scare me are things that might come up that could cause me to delay my success or make success more difficult to attain. I don't see that happening, but if it did, I would find a solution." That's a positive, confident, can-do attitude.

Stay positive, confident, and focused on what you can do for them. That's what will sell you for the job.

By the way... This question is a great time to introduce your 30-60-90-day plan. Talking about what you're excited about in this job is an ideal segue to what you've put together to be successful in your first 3 months on the job. And it's an amazing bridge for any experience gaps you might have, too.

What have you been doing
since you got laid off?

I know...this job interview question makes you want to roll your eyes. The painfully obvious answer is, "I've been trying to find a new job!" But you can't say that.

Why would they ask you this question? It turns out, they have several good reasons for asking. There are a lot of questions behind it, and if you know what they are, you can answer it more effectively. Here's what they're really asking:

"Are you able to maintain a positive attitude in a very difficult situation?" We all face difficulties in our lives and in our jobs. They want to know that you can keep going and find solutions even in the face of a difficult situation.

"How much of a go-getter are you when no one's watching?" Do you have the energy level required for this role? If you've just been lying around for several months while you're out of work, the answer is: probably not. If you got a good severance package when you got laid off and took some time for yourself, that's OK. But you should point out to them that you've only recently begun looking: "I've just recently begun my search for a new position, and here I am with you. I am really excited about a job opportunity like this one."

"Are you able to fill your time with constructive tasks when it seems you have nothing to do?" Are you a seeker? If you've been filling your time with retraining yourself or learning something new or even completing some family task you've always wanted to do, that's great and you should talk about it.

In fact, I always recommend that, in order to stay motivated for the job search, job seekers spend no more than 4-5 hours a day actively job searching. After that, do something that helps your mental or physical state: Volunteer, learn a new skill, take a class, and even work out. Job searching is tough and you should take care of yourself while you're in the process. I know of one guy who lost 50 pounds while he was out of work. Not only was that impressive, it did wonders for his attitude and mental outlook while he was job hunting.

All of those other things: volunteering, learning a new skill, or taking a class, are powerful signals to the hiring manager that you are someone who keeps striving. You are a go-getter and if she's smart, she'll jump at the chance to have a self-starter like you on her team.

Job Interview Question 63

What have you learned from your mistakes?

> **Anyone who has never made a mistake has never tried anything new.**
>
> — **Albert Einstein**

This job interview question is an opportunity for you to show them that you're a "growth" person...someone who learns from their mistakes and grows from it, developing into a stronger, smarter, better version of yourself.

If you want to keep it general, focus on universal truths or character traits. You can say that you've made mistakes in the past, and realized that there are certain universal tactics that are good to apply in any given situation: Evaluate exactly what's going on. Take in more than one opinion. Sleep on it. Don't make rash decisions. Be persistent. Show that you've matured and learned.

If they press you for an example, you need to be able to provide one, so you better have thought one up. And it should always end on a positive note.

Give your example in the form of a brief story. Use the STAR method to tell it...say what the Situation or Task you faced was, tell the Action you took that resulted in the mistake, and then go into the Results, or what you learned from it. And then take your story to the next level by telling them (if you can) about how you implemented what you learned in a different instance and succeeded. That gives you an even happier ending to your story.

A great story might sound like this: You tried something, it didn't go exactly right, you re-crafted it or made adjustments or did something different based on what you learned from the problems, and then you did it again and succeeded.

If you haven't had a chance to redo that situation with your new-found knowledge, then the story you tell is about what you learned from it and how and why you won't make that mistake again.

Both of these story structures will serve you well in the interview.

When you choose the specifics for your story, be strategic. Don't say anything damaging to the possibility of your performing well in this new role. Choose something that isn't so critical and then say what you learned.

One good example would be, "I made a mistake when I took my last job. I wasn't as critical as I should have been about what the job was really like, and when I got into it, it was completely different than what I should have pursued. Because of that, it cost me some time in my career, and it cost that company as well. I've learned to do quite a bit more research and ask more questions before I commit myself to a position."

Another might be, "I made a mistake when I was supposed to take a customer to X event, and I didn't send the final email. (Or, "I didn't give them my phone number", or whatever.) Because of that lack of communication, we missed the meeting. I learned to be meticulous about my customer communication, because very often it's those tiny details that make or break the whole thing."

http://careerconfidential.com

Job Interview Question 64

What is good customer service?

This question will generally be asked in interviews for retail or customer service jobs, but there's really a wide range of jobs that have contact with customers, or people who pay money for a good or service. Engineers, accountants, and manufacturers can have contact with customers, too.

I think that the best explanation of "good customer service" came from a recruiting client of mine who wanted to hire a good customer service rep. When I asked what that meant to them, they said, "Customer delight."

So in my opinion, the best answer to this question would sound like this: "Good customer service is that which delights the customer. It's what the customer says is good. It's not what you say is good. It's not what the company says is good. It's defined by the customer. The most important thing is to make the customer so happy that they will refer you to someone else. So one of the questions I always ask is, "Did I provide what you were looking for today?" because I know how vital it is to make sure I'm providing what they need so they will be delighted with us."

But any answer that indicates you're aware of how important 'customer delight' is would be fantastic. When you're speaking to a customer, you are the face of the company. You are their representative, you are in the front lines of their reputation in that arena. You matter a great deal.

Even a waitress needs to realize that she is the face of that restaurant. Diners don't see the people in the kitchen preparing their food, and they very often don't see the manager, either. They see the waitress. She has a profound impact on their experience at that restaurant, which will show up in how they feel about it, if they come back, and if they recommend it to others.

When I was in sales, I had a policy of treating every customer like I would treat my grandmother...politely, respectfully, and patiently. And I'm not a patient person. But I knew that if they had a good experience with me, they would buy from me again and they would tell others about me and my product. My customer service actions in the field would reflect in my sales numbers.

These attitudes are what you want to show the interviewer with your answer. Don't just say something like, "Good customer service is being friendly and helpful," or "Good customer service is being knowledgeable about my inventory and being able to help my customers make good decisions." Those aren't really bad answers, but you can do much better if you go one step further and talk about this idea of 'customer delight.'

Job Interview Question 65

What's Your Greatest Weakness?

"What's your greatest weakness?" is possibly the most annoying interview question just because of its sheer ridiculousness...your choices seem to be either to give them an obviously fake weakness (like you're a perfectionist or you work too hard...ugh!), or a real weakness (like you're disorganized or you have a bad temper), which means you might as well kiss your job offer goodbye now.

Most people stick with the safe route and go for the fake one. Do you? It turns out, the 'safe' route is not the best route.

The hiring manager's not just looking for your weakness. He doesn't really think you'll say something terrible about yourself. He's looking, among other things, at how you react to difficult. He knows that you know it's coming, so how prepared are you? And, the answer you choose will give him some insight into you and your personality.

YOU have the power to mold and shape this answer into one that serves you best (while sticking to the truth, of course).

There are several approaches, but this is the one I think will help you find your balance in this difficult answer:

Use an actual weakness that is also a strength in this job. A real weakness that might cause you a problem in other areas of your life but actually helps you achieve in this job. But for the most part, don't ever choose perfectionism, because it's too much of a cliché by now.

For instance, I always used impatience as my weakness. No one can argue that impatience isn't a real weakness. It is, and it's caused me problems. But impatience is also something that's driven me to succeed faster than other people. It's something that made me a better sales rep. I didn't want to wait for that sale, I was pushing to see if I could get it now.

Someone else could answer that they get frustrated with people who don't work as quickly as they do—which says that you work fast and are dedicated.

It seems more honest than talking about a weakness that you've overcome already—that's not your greatest weakness anymore, is it? But you absolutely can talk about ways you deal with and minimize the negative effects of the one you have.

Thinking about the greatest weakness question this way requires a little more creativity and thoughtfulness on your part, but the strategic advantages you'll gain from it in your interview will be worth it.

Job Interview Question 66

What is your ideal job?

In a personality test, this question may not be so easy to answer. But in a job interview, it's one of the easiest questions you'll be asked.

Question: What's your ideal job?

Answer: This one.

As far as they are concerned, your ideal job is the one you're interviewing for right now.

In asking this question, your interviewer is trying to find out if you'll be happy and productive in this position, with this company, or if you just want anything with a paycheck. So it's a little bit like answering the question, "Why do you want to work here?" They want to know that it's about more than the money.

So you can answer it from that point of view if you want. You can't actually be flip and say, "This one!" but you can talk about certain aspects of this job and how they fulfill personal goals and desires for you and that's why you got into this line of work and then tie it into why this particular job with this particular company is such a good fit for you.

This is yet another place where the company research you do before the interview will benefit you tremendously. If you've done your interview prep right, you can add those elements that make it clear that you are interested in this job, with this company.

"I really believe my ideal job is this one because I love X, Y, and Z, that's why I went into this area as a career. But I particularly am excited about this job with this company, because of what I've learned about how you handle ABC. It seems like an ideal environment to do what I love to do."

Or you could keep it more general and say something like:

My ideal job is one that I enjoy going to each day, where I can make an impact and be rewarded for it, and others notice that I'm making an impact and continue to grow in that way.

Do you see? You're talking about other rewards besides the money that make it worth it for you to get up and come to work every day. It shows that you're thoughtful and sincere and that you've thought about your fit for this role, which almost always means you'll be more successful.

Your answer here will speak to your enthusiasm for the job and ultimately, your success.

Job Interview Question 67

What is your least favorite managerial task?

With this question, they're trying yet again to get a feel for any potential weaknesses you'll bring to the job, without asking directly about your weaknesses. Hiring managers are fully aware that you'll be ready for the 'weakness' question, but maybe not so prepared for this one...so they hope they'll get an honest answer. Are you irritated by the details? Are you impatient with subordinates and their issues?

A side benefit for the interviewer is that your answer should also give them an idea of your management style. Are you task-oriented? Results-oriented? Focused on mentoring and developing your subordinates? What you don't like will give them a clue about what you do like and how you work.

If you get asked about your least favorite **anything** that has to do with your job, I sincerely hope you pick something that is a very small, insignificant part of your to-do list!

For instance, for a management role, you'd generally never want to say you dislike meetings (which are necessary for planning), filing reports (upper management needs to know what's going on), training employees (your job is to make them better), or sticking to a budget. Key responsibilities differ greatly depending on the job, so you had better do your homework and know very clearly what your job responsibilities will be so that you don't inadvertently say the wrong thing.

I once had a candidate say something that he hated that was actually a key part of his job. Obviously, he didn't get that position.

So, it's got to be a small part, and it's got to be something that everybody can see is distasteful. Here's an answer that I would give:

"For me, my least favorite task has always been firing people. I hate that. It doesn't mean that I would shy away from it if it had to be done, because we all have to do things we don't like to do for the sake of the organization or the goal, and you can make that clear in regard to yourself, too. You don't like it, but you will do the things that are necessary for the organization to be successful."

In fact, any task you choose as your least favorite should be immediately followed up with an acknowledgment of the necessity of doing even those tasks we don't enjoy in order to further the continued success of the organization. This will show your maturity and your professionalism.

http://careerconfidential.com

Job Interview Question 68

What kind of money would you be interested in making?

Hiring managers always want to know how much you're going to cost, so they'll ask the salary question a hundred different ways: "How much did you make at your last job?" "What are your salary expectations?" Or this one, "How much money do you want to make?" As much as you would like to say, "I'm interested in making as much money as I can!" you can't say that. Even if it's true. (Wouldn't we all?)

The truth is that for most jobs it doesn't matter so much how much you would be interested in making. This job has a range and it pays what it pays. It's up to you to do your salary research to find out what a reasonable salary range is for this particular position in this particular area of the country. If you have more experience or special skills that you're bringing to the party, you can reasonably expect to be on the high end of the scale. If you don't have that much experience, you're probably going to fall on the lower end.

The only exception would be in sales jobs that work entirely on commission. For those jobs, the salary range really is up to you, and your answer to this question needs to present you as a strong, energetic, driven, determined professional who is willing and able to do what it takes to make the sale and ring that cash register. They will love that answer because the more you make, the more they make. Your success will make your sales manager look great.

Still, the basic idea with all salary negotiation is to try to avoid being the first one to say an actual number. So when they ask you, "How much money do you want to make?" my first piece of advice is to turn it back to them and ask, "What is the salary range you have budgeted for this position?" If they tell you, you can say, "That seems like a reasonable range for this job. If we agree that I'm the best fit for the position, I would be comfortable with an offer in that range."

If they don't let it go and instead press you for an answer, you can say, "I've done some research and I understand that the going rate for this job falls somewhere between X and Y dollars. Is that the range you're offering?" You're still dodging a number, and asking a question that throws it back in their laps. If they tell you that in fact, it is what they're offering, you can again offer reassurance that you would be comfortable with that range if you agree that you're the person for the job.

What makes you unique?

What are hiring managers really asking when they ask about what makes you unique? Well, they don't want to know about what makes you special on a personal level. They want to know what makes you unique in relation to the job you're interviewing for. Essentially, they're asking, "Why should we hire you?" "Why should we choose you over everyone else?" "What makes you different from the other candidates?"

What makes you unique is your individual blend of education, experiences, skill sets, and personality. Sometimes it's not the particular job on your resume that makes you appeal to hiring managers. Sometimes it's an aggregate of the different pieces that you're bringing to the table. Maybe you have strong communication skills, and experience in the industry, and experience in advertising and that ends up being the mix that attracts that hiring manager to you.

Think about what makes you unique and what makes you valuable, and then think about WHY it makes you valuable. You can even quantify your answer of how in the past, your blend of experiences has proven valuable to previous employers.

"Because of my background in X, I was uniquely positioned to take advantage of Y when I worked on ABC project. I completed it faster and with better results than anyone else in the company."

"I believe that my education in X combined with my experience in Y work together to give me an especially great advantage when approaching ABC. I draw on both to solve both every day issues and special challenges. For example, in X Situation, I took Y action and got Z results."

"My background in X is different from most people in the field, and that gives me a unique perspective and the ability to see solutions that are more creative and resourceful. For example, I came up with X solution to solve Y problem, and it worked out beautifully." (A few numbers that prove that success would be outstanding to include here.)

If the quality or the success rate of your work is outstanding, that's valuable to an employer because it saves them time, money, and aggravation. But you have to think about why it is that you are especially successful and be able to articulate that.

Whatever you say, now is the time to brag. You must show that your particular blend of education, experiences, skill sets and personality is the solution they need to solve the problems they have.

http://careerconfidential.com

Job Interview Question 70

What motivates you?

What's the one big elephant in the room that MUST be ignored with the motivation question? All together now: "Money."

As much as the money question is a big part of why you work, employers want to think that you're also doing this because you love it. And you should love it. You can make money doing a lot of different things, so you should enjoy the job you choose to do.

The reason hiring managers ask this question is that they want to know what makes you tick and that you have your own reasons for working hard and achieving goals that have nothing to do with them and the paycheck. People who are motivated by some other force than the direct monetary reward work harder and do better at their jobs.

To answer this classic job interview question, be strategic and relate what motivates you to your skill set and your fit for the job. This is an ideal place to show your enthusiasm for the work, and that's very appealing to hiring managers.

A great answer strategy is to try to think about some project that you really enjoyed and pinpoint what it is that really motivated you to work on it and do a good job. Talk about the project and what you enjoyed about it, and how it relates to something that you'd be doing in this job.

If you're in project management, talk about how you love to orchestrate the process of a successful project and see all the different parts and pieces come together to a conclusion and then name a complicated project you worked on, talk briefly about the challenges of it, and tell how it turned out.

If you're in sales, talk about how you are motivated by a sales target because you are so competitive. And then tell about how you met and exceeded your sales numbers last year.

If you are in customer service, talk about how you love to uncover a customer's needs, solve their problem and end the interaction on a positive note. And then you could maybe throw in an example of a particularly difficult customer issue that you solved.

Bottom line: Keep your answer positive and use it to point to a significant accomplishment.

If you do that, you can hit two birds with one stone: You can sell your enthusiasm for the job along with your skill and fit.

http://careerconfidential.com

Job Interview Question 71

What questions do you have for us?

By the end of the interview, when they ask if you have any questions for them, you probably feel like you're toast. You're just done, and you want to go home. That's the way most people feel, so the most common response to this question is, "I don't have any questions, I think you've covered everything."

That's bad, bad, bad. It's one of the things you should never say in a job interview. It makes you look uninterested in the job.

The best questions to ask are those that make it clear you've been listening to what their main problems and concerns are. Clarify, elaborate, or dig deeper. There are lots of good questions to ask.

You can ask about the timeline: "How soon do you want to have someone in the role?" That shows you are motivated to get started quickly.

You can ask about the last person who was in this role. If the person who had the position before was promoted, ask, "Is that a traditional track for this job?" If the person who was in the role before wasn't meeting expectations, ask, "Can you tell me how they weren't meeting expectations so I could understand?"

If you're speaking with your direct future boss, ask about the biggest challenges of the job and can he see you meeting those challenges?

If you're speaking with the Human Resources Manager, ask about the company, the growth of the department, where it fits in relation to the rest of the company, and so on.

If you're speaking with upper management, ask questions that demonstrate your understanding of the industry as a whole and this company's place in it and its plans for the future.

This is not the time to ask about anything that would benefit you, like salary, vacations, or perks. At this point, they're like your customer. It's all about them right now, not you. Remember that the job interview is a sales process and you have to keep selling, or keep showing them all the different reasons why you'd be a good fit for them until they say, "yes, we want to hire you." You don't have to keep asking an endless round of more and more questions. Just ask a few more questions that show your interest, enthusiasm, and concern for their problem (which is the job that isn't getting done until they put someone in that role).

Continue the conversation and ask questions to find out more details that will help you move in the direction of uncovering more of their motivations, needs, and wants you can so you can better position yourself as the candidate they want.

http://careerconfidential.com

Job Interview Question 72

What salary are you looking for?

I hope that you know beyond a shadow of a doubt that you are never to bring up money in the interview, at any time, until they make you an offer—until they say, "yes, you're the one, let's come to terms." Curbing your enthusiasm until then will serve you in the end.

Bringing up money too soon is a job interview mistake. You'll look like the paycheck is all you care about, and that's a big turnoff for hiring managers, understandably. And if you wait until they feel like they've got to have you, then the money conversation ends up being a lot more in your favor. People are usually willing to pay a little more for a product they're already sold on.

However, it's pretty common for the interviewer to try to pin you down on salary before you get to that point. They are very interested in how much you're going to cost by asking about your salary expectations as soon as they can. It's only natural for them to want to find out as much as they can, but if you let go of that too soon, it can hurt your salary negotiations later.

As in most job interview situations, you've got a couple of good options:

You can try to deflect with some humor by asking: "Does that mean you're making me an offer?"

You can turn the question back to them and say: "What's the range you have set for this position?" When they tell you, you can say, "I'm comfortable with that. If you decide that I'm a good fit for the job and I decide it's a good fit for me, I will be completely fine with discussing a salary in that range."

Or you can be more straightforward and say, "I'm really interested in finding out more about the job and telling you more about me so that we can see if we're a good fit before we start talking about the money."

If that doesn't feel comfortable, you can say, "I'm looking for a great opportunity, and I'm sure you'll offer a salary that's commensurate with the responsibility of this job."

What all of these answers do is help you deflect the question. You want to do overall is to put that discussion off for as long as possible.

You want the focus to be on selling yourself for the job—because if they don't want to hire you, the money doesn't matter anyway. You don't have anything to talk about, really, until they're ready to say yes to hiring you.

http://careerconfidential.com

Job Interview Question 73

What type of work environment do you prefer?

The best answer to this job interview question of what work environment do you prefer is the same answer you'd give to "What's your ideal job?" The correct answer is: "This one."

Of course, you need to respond with the type of work environment that they have, or at least close to it, or you're not going to get the job.

But, you don't just want to get the offer...you want to get a job that fits you as well.

Since you don't know exactly what their work environment is like, it's best to answer by talking about how flexible you are, and then following that up with "What would you say the environment is here?" Or, "How would you describe the environment here?"

Here's a good, positive example:

"I have preferred [X-type] of environment in the past, but I love new experiences and what I can learn from them. I see a different type of environment as a new way to develop additional skills. What would you say the work environment is like here?"

The work environment could be fast-paced, technology-based, customer-focused, high-tech, internet-based, retail-based...it could be anything. Maybe they'll say that they are very creative and loose, or highly-structured, or like nothing you've ever seen before.

When they tell you, you'll get either (a) a really good idea that you're going to hate this job and it's a good thing you found out now; or (b) certain words or phrases from them that will make you say, "I thrive in that type of environment."

With a better idea of the type of work environment they have, you can elaborate on your answer to talk about how you are so enthusiastic about being able to be a part of that, or how you have done well in other environments like theirs, and therefore expect to do well in theirs, too.

The job interview really isn't just a hurdle for you to cross in order for you to get the job. It's really supposed to be a way for both parties to get to know one another. They want to know if you're going to fit in, be happy and do well there. Hiring you is an expensive proposition for them, and a risk. Can you do the job? Are you going to be happy in their company culture? And you need to know if this is a place you'll be happy to spend a large portion of your waking time, and if it will be good for your long-term career. This question is a way to have that necessary conversation.

Job Interview Question 74

What was the last book you read?

It doesn't matter if the last book you read was an actual paper variety with a spine and real pages or the digital version on your Kindle. If you read on a regular basis, it usually means that you're someone who's intelligent, curious, and interested in personal growth and learning. It also usually means you're a good communicator. For some interviewers, that's all they want to know. For others, they are hoping you'll indicate that you're keeping up with the reading in your field...that you're on top of trends, or the latest information. There are so many things we can learn from reading and it's a big plus for most people and most jobs.

The first rule when answering this question is: Do not lie about the last book you read. Ever. Do not name a book unless you have read it. I once interviewed someone who did lie about it and it was horrible. I caught him in the lie because I had just read the book he named. When I asked him what he thought about something in the book, of course he couldn't tell me and was completely embarrassed, and it left me wondering what else he was lying about.

Anticipate that you might get this question and think about a book you can read and talk about. Think about that book a little bit before you go into the interview because you might just get someone like me who reads a lot and will want to discuss it with you.

Ideally, you can talk about a book that pertains to your job or your industry. It can be something you read just for enjoyment, but try not to name a romance novel, "Fifty Shades of Grey," anything from the "Twilight" series, or anything you might be embarrassed to be seen with in front of your more "educated" friends. It won't make the interviewer see you the way you need to be seen in order to look good in the interview and get this job offer.

I think that one of the best things you can do for your career, and especially in your job search, is to read books that will help you be more knowledgeable about your field. Something that will help you be better than you were before. My best advice is to go find some of those books and start reading. It will give you some interesting material for your next interview.

http://careerconfidential.com

Job Interview Question 75

What was your least favorite part of your last job?

Why does the hiring manager want to know about your least favorite part of your last job? Because they want to find out more about you, and they are hoping to uncover any potential problems before they hire you. What you say and the way you say it will tell them a lot more than you think.

The basic job interview strategy you want to follow with answering this question is to keep the emphasis on the positive rather than the negative, and be logical (strategic). Don't tell them something you didn't like that you will find in this job. Don't give them a reason not to hire you.

You never want to go too negative with this answer, either, even though it's about things you don't like. Something like, "I didn't like my manager," or "I didn't get along with my co-workers" is always bad because of what it says about you, that maybe you're the one who's difficult to get along with. You never want to talk about how the workload was killing you, even if it really was unreasonable, because it makes you look like you can't handle the job.

But the answer has to be something you didn't like, so try to make sure it is not something that's a factor in this job. If you didn't like that you had no opportunities for promotion, make sure that there are advancement opportunities in the new job. If you weren't given the chance to be creative, make sure there's plenty of creativity built into this job. If you weren't challenged, say, "I didn't have as much of a chance as I wanted to use my skills in X, Y, and Z and expand my knowledge in this field. That's why I'm so looking forward to being able to utilize those skills and grow and develop into greater responsibility here."

Maybe you could even talk about things outside of the job, like "my last job required me to drive an hour every day to get there, and that commute really cuts into my day. This job is just a few minutes from my house. Not only am I really excited about the job itself, but I'm also excited about being so close and getting rid of that commute."

So, the bottom line is, don't make it personal. Give them an answer of something that will automatically change as a result of you getting this job.

Job Interview Question 76

What was your most difficult work experience and how did you deal with it?

This is a great opportunity to talk about how you've overcome a challenge and ended up a winner! You can talk about how you stepped up to a difficult situation and got a good outcome, or how you overcame something that was holding you back in your job (maybe you learned a new skill).

Because this is a classic behavioral interview question, you want to use the STAR format to talk about this: Describe the Situation or Task (what was going on), the Action you took (what you did) and the Result (what happened). You can also talk about how you would do it differently if you had it to do over.

Basically, you want to describe this difficult work experience, how you analyzed it, how you possibly brought in other resources to solve it, and how it turned out OK. And if you can quantify, it's even better. What do I mean when I say "quantify"?

Quantifying your answer just means adding numbers, dollars, or percentages to your description of it. So instead of saying "I improved sales," you're going to say, "I improved sales by 30%".

"I wrote customer emails," becomes "I wrote customer emails that brought in 10 new customers per month."

"I was known for delivering all my projects on time" becomes

"My project delivery was 100% on time."

"I was a top student in my class" becomes "I ranked #2 in a class of 400, with a 3.9 GPA."

It's much more powerful and attention-getting to add those numbers, dollars, and percentages to your accomplishments. You're saying the same thing, but with more preciseness. You're adding evidence. This is a skill you need to know for both your interview answers and your resume, too. Numbers matter.

Then, your answer sounds more like: "Once, I faced X situation. It was a big problem because of ABC. I realized that our biggest obstacle was Y, so I put some thought into it [you'd want to say what that thought process was here] and decided to do Z. It worked out really well. Because of that, we saw a revenue jump of $10,000 that month."

But it doesn't have to be dollars. It could be that you saved time, increased accuracy, decreased loss, increased customer numbers (without naming dollar amounts), or anything that you can describe by saying "how many" or "how much." That's the way to end your answer and be more impressive in the interview.

http://careerconfidential.com

Job Interview Question 77

What were the major challenges of your last job and how did you handle them?

> **Sometimes adversity is what you need to face in order to become successful.**
> **– Zig Ziglar**

This is a tough job interview question to answer because the major challenges of your last job typically are going to be the key job skills that you're bringing to the new one. (The exception being if you're a brand new graduate or transitioning careers). Since most jobs you interview for build on the job you had before, you're actually likely to be talking about the job skills that you're going to take on in this new role.

You always want to be positive about your job skills. If you successfully dodged the weakness question, you don't want to get caught in this one.

The idea you want to go with here is to talk about a few of the major situational challenges you faced in your last role that you handled successfully—using your key job skills, if possible. Or, you could even choose a challenge that you dealt with using your key job skills, plus some other supplementary skill that you bring to the table that makes you a unique and valuable employee.

You want to use the STAR format to put it together. (STAR stands for Situation or Task, Action you took, and Results you got.)

There's nothing magic about the format. It just ensures that you give a complete answer, and that you end on a positive note: a result.

First, explain what the challenge was and why it was important. Then take them through your thought process: Did you have to research new information? Did you have to call in additional resources? What resources did you bring in? Then, tell them how it ended up. If you can quantify your result, do it.

If you can, choose challenges that highlight the top skills they want someone to have in this role. You can have a story or two in your mind when you go to the interview if you are very familiar with the job description and the company. (This is yet another reason to do your homework and research the job and the company before you interview.)

With all behavioral interview questions, the hiring manager wants to know how you handled a past situation so that he can see how you might handle a future similar situation. Keep this story positive, don't badmouth anyone when telling it, and focus on the results you got from your actions.

Job Interview Question 78

What were your responsibilities in your last job?

Your answer to this question about your job responsibilities depends entirely on the role you played in your last job. What were your major responsibilities? You want to list those out.

A reasonable person might think, "Why would they ask about the responsibilities of my last job? It says right there on my resume what my last job was." The trouble is that job titles and the actual work they entail don't always match up the way you think they're going to. One company's Customer Support Specialist might have entirely different duties than another's. Or maybe you would assume that a Manager might do certain things based on that title, but in reality, they don't in that company. It's best never to assume. So they ask. And they want to see your perception of your job, too.

It's a good thing that they do ask, because this is a great opportunity for you to point out what a great fit you are for this job.

Start with the biggest responsibility you had, or the one that is most relevant to the job you're interviewing for. Because you want to sell yourself, right? How you present yourself in the interview is all up to you. Choose wisely the responsibilities you talk about.

So if this role is an operations role, you want to start talking about your operations responsibilities.

If it's a finance role, you want to talk about your finance responsibilities.

You want to make that connection to what matters to this manager. Pick the top 3 or 4 responsibilities, briefly talk about them and say, "I believe that's one of the reasons why I'm a great fit for this job. What I've done before is very similar to what I'd be doing for you. I've been very successful at it, and I can be successful for you, too."

If you've done your research and carefully read the job requirements, this should be easy.

What if your previous job wasn't similar to this one? Well, then, now is the time for you to show your transferable skills. Something you did in your old job developed a skill you can use in this new one. When you answer, connect those dots for the hiring manager and sell yourself for the job.

One warning: Don't lie about your previous job responsibilities. The hiring manager can and most likely will check your references, and when they do, you will be caught. Besides, the best way to prove that you can do the job even though you haven't before is not a lie, it is a 30/60/90-day plan. That's very convincing evidence that you've got what it takes for the job.

What will you contribute to this job?

This question is very similar to "Why should we hire you?" Or, "Why do we want you over the other candidates?" The job interview is a sales process in which you are the product and the hiring manager and company is the buyer. Your salary is the price of the product, you and your skill sets. It's fair for them to ask, "What are we going to get for our money?"

If they ask you what you'll contribute, rejoice. This is a softball question. It's an ideal time to sell yourself for the job. If you get this, you're golden.

So how do you approach it? You want to be thinking about what they've asked for in the job description. You should have already connected your skill sets to what they're asking for in this role. You can also get some priceless additional insight into what they're looking for when you ask questions during the interview.

One great question to ask early on in the interview is, "What does your ideal candidate look like?" They'll give you a wish list that might include things that aren't in the description. Take in all that information and talk about how you have what they're looking for plus a little extra. That "plus a little extra" is important.

They're already looking at candidates who meet their requirements. Show them how you meet and exceed those requirements. Maybe that's more experience, additional background that allows you to bring a different perspective, or character traits like your strong work ethic or driven personality. That's "extra" is what's going to set you apart as a unique candidate. Sum that up in a positive way that sells you for the job.

This is also an ideal time to bring out your **30/60/90-day plan.** This plan is an outline for what you will do in the first 3 months on the job. It covers any on-the-job training, getting up to speed, and how you'll become a fully-functioning employee. Hiring managers love these things because they show that you are someone who goes the extra mile and can put some critical thought into the job and how you'll be successful at it. They say, "What will you contribute?" And you say, "I'm so glad you asked. I've written up a plan that shows you how I will bring myself up to speed quickly in the job and start contributing by doing X, Y, and Z." And then you've launched into that conversation, which will elevate your interview conversation in a big way.

What will you do if you don't get this position?

This question is mostly likely to be asked when you're interviewing for an internal job or promotion. You're probably going up against other candidates in the company, and maybe even some external candidates, too. They're worried about how you'll take it if you don't get the job, and they want to know if you're more interested in the good of the company or just in your own career advancement.

If this is the case, a good answer would tell them that you're a team player who is interested in the good of the company.

For example: "Of course, I will support whoever you choose to fill this position, and I'll keep doing the great job I always do. But I do think that I'm a great fit for this role because of X, Y, and Z, and that I would be the best choice." (A bad answer would be: "I'll assume that you're never going to appreciate me and I'll be looking for someone who does.")

However, you might get asked this question in a regular job interview, where you're new to the company. Maybe they're fishing to see where else you're applying, maybe they want to know how serious you are about your job search. You don't need to tell them where else you're applying, but by all means let them know that you are committed to getting a new job and that you will be a great asset for someone somewhere. Here's an example:

"I would really like to get the job here, because I think I'm a great fit. I'm excited about your company because of the work you do in A, B, and C. But if I don't get the job, I'm going to go on living and breathing, and I'm going to find someone else who's going to appreciate my skill sets, and I'm going to get to work doing what I do best. They're going to really appreciate it, and I'm going to drive their business." (Or increase their productivity, reduce their costs, increase their market share, improve their customer service, whatever it is that would apply in your situation.)

You're going to do all those great things in a role similar to this one in another company. You'd like for it to be here, but if not, it will be somewhere else. You are that determined. You are going to get a job.

That's a strong, positive answer that shows that you are confident in yourself and your abilities.

Job Interview Question 81

What would you do first at this job?

When they ask you this question in the interview, they want to get a picture of how you would be in the role. How you answer tells them about your personality and your work style. Do you attack it from day one? Do you take it all in and analyze it first?

If it were me, I would answer it like this: "The first thing I would do is get to know all the systems and parts and pieces I need to know in order to be successful at the job. I would want to define what my end goal was and then work backwards from there and make sure that I know everything I need to be successful at this."

And then I would introduce my 30/60/90-day plan: "I'm glad you asked that, because I have been doing a lot of thinking about this question and I came up with a working list of what I would do in the first 3 months. Can I get your input on that to see if I'm on the right track?"

A 306090-day plan is a written outline for what you will do in your first 3 months on the job. It covers any training you need, learning about the company, getting up to speed, and launching off on your own great things. It's very impressive to hiring managers because it shows your knowledge of the job, your drive, energy, and initiative, and your commitment to success.

Using your plan, you walk them though your thought process and you have your discussion about your first 90 days on the job. You talk, you ask questions, they clarify, and you become cemented in their minds as a fantastic candidate. This discussion is guaranteed to be a more in-depth, better conversation about you in that role than any standard list of job interview questions and answers will allow you to have.

(Even if you chicken out and don't bring your actual plan into the interview, you still should do the interview prep work of creating a plan, so that you have something solid to say in answer to this question. They're that good for preparing you and transforming you into the most knowledgeable candidate.)

Just walk them through what you think would make you successful on the job, and ask questions as you go that confirm it and keep you on the right track.

http://careerconfidential.com

Job Interview Question 82

What would your friends tell me about you?

This question could also easily be "What would your friends or co-workers tell me about you?" They just want to know what you would say about how other people would describe you.

Asking you about what your friends would tell the interviewer about you seems like an odd question, doesn't it? But there are lots of reasons an interviewer might ask it: (1) they want to know how you will potentially get along with your co-workers; (2) they want to see if what you say makes sense with what they're seeing in you during the interview; and (3) they're just looking for more of your personality to see if you're going to be a good cultural fit for the company.

If it were me, I would say, "My friends would tell you the same thing my references would tell you: that I'm high-energy, I'm competitive, and I'm driven to succeed. I have those same qualities in my personal life as I do in my professional life." Those happen to be great qualities for someone in sales (as I was).

Just choose 3 or 4 positive traits you possess that would be a plus for someone in that job. That's part of a good job interview strategy. Always be able to tie your answer back to something that would recommend you for the job.

Other great qualities employers might be looking for? Reliable, dedicated, hard-working, honest, organized, trustworthy, efficient, positive, dynamic, strategic, detail-oriented, motivated, self-starter, calm, caring, empathetic, loyal, a leader, professional, flexible, adaptable, a quick learner. It depends on you and your job.

The key: Be consistent. Don't say something that your references will contradict. Either the interviewer will notice the distinct lack of a similar response in your references, or they might even just come out and ask, "Do you think Suzie is someone who ___?" And if they get a long pause as a response, you have just damaged your chances very badly.

Here's a hint: Go back though your performance appraisals and look for descriptive words there. An even better idea is to pick a few trusted people (mentors, previous bosses, past or current co-workers) and ask them what impression you give to others. What 3 words would they choose to describe you? You have to be a little bit brave with this one. It can be a difficult question to ask. But the answers you get will help you both answer this question and help you make sure you are projecting the image you want to project in this job search.

Job Interview Question 83

What would your manager say was the area you needed most development in?

This question might also sound like, "What would your boss say you need to improve on?" No doubt about it...impressing your boss is always important, and we all have things about ourselves that we could improve on. As with all interview questions, be thoughtful and strategic with how you answer it.

This question is an obvious effort to find out more about your weaknesses, so think about it like the weakness question. There are several strategies you can take: name a real weakness that would be irrelevant for this job, or name a strength that could be even better.

If you name a weakness, it must be something that won't matter or have an effect on your performance in this job, and it's even better if the weakness is something that helps you in your job even though it might hold you back in your personal life.

If you name a strength, it must not be an essential strength you need for good performance on this job.

For instance, if you are a project manager, obviously you wouldn't say you needed better organizational skills. But you also don't want to say that you could have better communication skills. That's a pretty big deal for someone who coordinates people, things, and deadlines. Maybe you would say that you needed to improve on your patience, as in, you sometimes get impatient with the pace of progress, because you are so focused on getting the job done.

In my case, I would say something about needing more detail-management (not a factor in whether or not I make the sale, but also something that nearly everyone could benefit from some improvement in), but then I would talk about the steps I am currently taking to either correct or eliminate that as an issue—organizational software, a great app, something. Talk about how you are correcting the problem, and then give an instance where the steps you are taking worked.

If you are lucky enough that your current boss is going to be one of your references, one great strategy is to get with him or her ahead of time and go over what they might say in response to general job interview questions about your strengths, your weaknesses, your greatest accomplishments, etc. Prepping your references before the interview is a fantastic, proactive thing to do. And in this particular instance, you can make sure you're on the same page so that your answers don't conflict.

http://careerconfidential.com

Job Interview Question 84

What can you do to make this company better?

There are a million ways for an interviewer to ask "Why should we hire you?" and this is one of them. They want to know what benefits you as an employee are bringing to the table, and it's right for them to ask. The job interview is where you sell yourself for the job. That doesn't mean you have to act like a stereotypical salesman...it just means that you need to know what the needs of this company are...what problems they have that you can solve. And then you have to be able to articulate to them how you can solve them...how you've solved them before, how you've solved similar problems, how you perform in similar situations.

This question is a great place for you to be strategic in your answer. You want to start with the job itself and with your conversation with them about their biggest problems and what they need help with...or what they need changed or what they need a solution for. And hopefully somewhere in your conversation you've asked them what their biggest concerns are for this position and what their biggest goals are. Remind them that you're first going to attack those problems and come up with solutions for them.

And then you say, that's the first way I'll make the company better, because when I take care of those A, B, C things that we talked about, that makes D, E, and F better for you. And then that affects G, H, and I.

So just by doing those things, I'm going to have a positive ripple effect on the company and as I learn more and expand my responsibilities, I will be able to positively impact the company in other ways.

You're painting a verbal picture for them so that they can see you in the job with all the benefits and positive impact you'll bring to the organization in a variety of ways.

You can do this in just your conversation, but this is really an ideal spot to introduce your30/60/90-day plan, and that will make you into an even stronger candidate, whether you have experience or not. A written-out plan for what you're going to do in the first 90 days will show them that you are someone who can size up a situation, analyze it, and create a plan of action to reach your goals. That's an incredibly impressive skill, and if you go to that much trouble before you even get the job, they will be amazed.

Job Interview Question 85

Where do you see yourself in 5 years?

In other words, are you going to bail on them in a few months for another job, or stick around and make their training and investment in you pay off? Is this a stepping stone on your career path, or a job to pay the bills until you can do what you really want to do?

This is a tough question. It's difficult to predict that far ahead, and plans change anyway. They do want to hear that you plan to stick around for a while and grow and develop with the company. If you're an "over 50" candidate, don't say that you'll be thinking about retirement. You want to give the impression that you are still looking forward to learning and growing and working, not looking forward to golf.

Many, many people believe that the best answer is some version of: "I see myself in your job!" or, "I want to be in management" because they think it shows ambition. That is not always the best answer.

If you're interviewing with a very large company, it might be just fine for you to talk about your desire to be promoted and to grow within the company. There's room for you to do that in a large corporation.

But if you are interviewing with a smaller company, an answer like that just might be considered a threat to that person's job. If they don't have anywhere to go, they're certainly not going to let you push them out.

A much better answer (in both situations, really) is to say something more along the lines of "I want to grow and develop my skills," or "I want to be all I can be." You can talk about how you look forward to greater responsibility as you learn more about the company, and that you hope to be ready to do more things. Then you can say, "If you are looking at me for a management position at that time, I would be interested in it, but that's not necessarily my end goal. What I really want out of this is to learn, to grow, and to contribute in a meaningful way."

There is no hiring manager who won't be impressed by a strategic job interview answer like that.

Job Interview Question 86

Who was your best boss and who was your worst?

This question tests several things about you and gives a lot of information to the interviewer:

- Are you adaptable?
- Can you get along with a wide variety of people?
- Do you carry grudges?
- Do you fit their company's cultural style?
- Do you fit your potential hiring manager's leadership?
- How do you react to negative situations?

Your overall goal to keep in mind is to stay positive and communicate that you can work with any boss in any situation.

To do that, you can't get too specific in what you expect in a supervisor when you talk about how great a particular boss was. If your potential boss for this job doesn't match what you say, you won't get hired. At the same time, you can't start in on how bad one boss was. Even if you can tell a story that has people howling with laughter at parties, you can't tell that story here. Any hint of negativity only makes you look like a negative person to the interviewer.

A great answer in response to "Who was your best boss?" sounds something like, "I've been so lucky to have had some great bosses that I've learned a lot from. They have all had some characteristic or habit or knowledge that I've been able to learn so much from." And then maybe you can say something you learned from one boss in particular that touches directly on your fit for this job: maybe it's a skill or a habit or something that makes you extremely good at what you do.

A great response for "Who was your worst boss?" sounds more like, "I did have a boss who I inherited. I didn't choose him and he didn't choose me and our communication styles were very different. We got along OK and I succeeded with him but it wasn't like it was with other managers."

Why is that a good response? Because you've chosen something vague enough that it won't come back to bite you in this interview, and you kept the outcome positive (meaning you hold no grudges, it was just one of those things, and you were still successful). You never want to badmouth a previous boss.

Try to spin any negative experience into a positive learning experience for you that made you better or stronger than you were before, that you will carry right into this new job.

Why are you looking to leave your current job?

It's very important that you think about this well before you set foot in an interview. Interviewers always want to know why, and you must have a good answer ready to go.

This can be a delicate subject, because most people don't leave a job that's a positive situation for them. The sticking point is that you never want to appear negative about anything in a job interview because it reflects so badly on you, so you absolutely can't say anything negative in this answer. This is not where you start talking about all the things you don't like about your current job or your current boss. First of all, it doesn't matter, and second of all, it will only make you look like a whiny complainer to this person. And it will make them think, "Wow, if he'll dish all this dirt about them, what will he say about us?"

If you must give a reason, make sure it's something neutral (by 'neutral' I mean: not negative) that is a factor in your old job and is not a factor in your new one.

For instance, if this job requires no travel, you could say, "There's a lot of travel in the old job and I'm ready to be at home in my own bed more often."

Or you could say, if you're moving from a small company to a big one: "I've loved my time at XYZ Company and learned many skills, but there's just not much room for growth at higher levels there and I'm ready to move up."

Or if the new job is in another city, you can say, "I hate to leave that company; they've been very good to me, but I am moving to this area and need something that's closer to home."

Be as brief as you can. Mostly what you want to do here is focus on how it's not that you're running away from that job, it's that you're running to this job. And give them a reason you're running to this job: it is such a great fit, it offers so many things you're looking for, and so on... Be as specific as you can about what it is that you're running to with this company. Why do you like them? Why is it a great fit for you? Tell them that, and you'll have a great answer.

http://careerconfidential.com

Job Interview Question 88

Why did you freelance for so long?

A lot of people have taken up freelancing, consulting, or other independent work in the last few years just out of necessity. In many industries, it's been difficult to find a job. Others have struck out on their own because there has been just so much opportunity—especially in consulting, writing, graphic design, web programming, web, and online marketing. Whatever your situation was, employers are going to have questions about your reasons for doing what you did and consequently, why you want to work for their company now. Do your job interview prep and be ready.

Whatever you do, **don't** give an answer like these:

- "I liked it, but I need insurance."
- "No one would hire me, so I did what it took to make money."
- "I didn't really have to work because my spouse made enough money, but now we're getting divorced."

Why are those bad answers? Because they show you running away from a bad situation, not running to their job. No one ever wants to be the consolation prize, and that includes employers. If you don't really want to be there, chances are you're not going to put in your best work.

You want to show that things were just fine and that you aren't being forced to work for them. This is your choice.

For example, say something like, "Frankly I got caught up in it. Things were going well, there really wasn't a problem. I just decided that I would be better served to be in an organization like this one."

And then you can give your reasons for wanting to work for them. Why is that company a good fit for you? Start by giving them a reason that fits your professional skills (maybe you realize how much better you could be with the right resources and infrastructure). Then give them a reason that you personally like the company. This would be a cultural fit reason. You don't have to work just anywhere, you want to work for them because they fit you well. The third reason can be more of a personal reason: you're looking forward to collaborating with people and feeding off each other's ideas so that you can be better and stronger than you've ever been.

The big point you must communicate is that you are not leaving a failing situation. You are excited about bringing your skills and talents to a larger organization and looking forward to the prospect.

Job Interview Question 89

Why did you leave your last position?

The underlying questions behind "Why did you leave your last position?" are, "Is there something wrong with you?" "Did you get fired for a reason?" "Will I regret hiring you?" Those are the concerns that you need to address when you answer this question.

It's important that you don't say anything negative about the company you were with because any negativity reflects very badly on you, but you still have to give them a reason why you're no longer with that company. Your answer will depend on what happened, but there are ways you can talk about it to put a positive spin on it.

If you were laid off, and you can truthfully say that it was a mass layoff, like they laid off 40% of the sales force, or they laid off 10% of the workforce and the newest employees went first, then say that. It will make them feel better to know that it wasn't just you. They will understand a mass layoff situation, because so many companies have cut back on their numbers the last few years.

If you weren't part of a mass layoff—maybe it was a restructuring, maybe it was just a much smaller number of people, it's very important that you be able to offer references who can speak to your skills and your character. The very best reference in this situation is your old boss. That will ease a lot of doubt.

If that's not possible because you were in fact fired, don't try to act like you weren't. They will almost certainly call your references and your old company to find out the truth. You can say something like, "I have to be honest with you here. That was kind of a bad situation that I'm embarrassed about. It wasn't a good decision to take that job—I did it for the wrong reasons, it wasn't a good fit, etc. I can only say that it was a brief bump in the road of an otherwise great career. I would love to have you speak to some of my references, including my former employer John Smith (who is going to be your boss from a job you've had in the past). They will be able to speak to my qualifications for this job, and my work ethic."

And then make sure you prep and coach those references. They need to know they're about to get a phone call, and they need to know what's most important for them to speak about. Your references are an ideal resource for you to utilize in this particular situation.

http://careerconfidential.com

Why did you take a job that seems to be outside of your career path?

So what happens when your potential employer is reading through your resume and they come across the job that doesn't make sense? You have a job in your history that doesn't fall within the logical progression of jobs in your field. And they want to know why.

What they're looking for here is at least some thought process...some understanding of who you are and where you're going. Why did you take that job? What they are afraid of is that you don't know what you want to do and if they hire you, you might not want to hang around their company very long, either. The hiring and onboarding process is disruptive to companies, and most want to minimize turnover so they can concentrate on making money.

There are actually a lot of valid reasons you could have taken an odd job that don't reflect badly on you and will make sense to them: Maybe you thought that industry experience was going to be really useful; maybe you thought that you could learn a lot from that boss; maybe you thought that skill set you'd pick up there would be a benefit to you. Going after additional skills is a positive. Or, maybe the truth is that you had no other choice: you needed a good job, and this was one. Sometimes practicality is reason enough. Just explain that you have worked your tail off in that job, but now it's time to move on to one that more closely fits your skill sets or your desired outcome as far as a career path goes.

They're looking for you to make them feel better about something that puzzles them. And unless you answer that question where they do feel better about it, you have not done a good job of representing yourself in the interview. So you really need to think this through and put yourself in the shoes of the hiring manager.

Just explain to them what they want to know: Are you being thoughtful about your career? Are you making good decisions? Or are you just impulsively taking any old job that sounds good? Why did you do this? And most importantly, does that have anything to do with why you want this job? Are you going to be happy in this career long-term?

Tell them why you made that decision, tell them what you learned from it, and then come back around to why you'd be a good fit for this job.

Job Interview Question 91

Why do you believe you are the best fit for this position?

This job interview question closely resembles "Why should we hire you?" It's one question that makes candidates very uncomfortable because it puts them on the spot, but it's really a fantastic question. Why? It allows you free rein to sell.

Remember that every job interview is a sales process. You are the product (and the sales rep), and the hiring manager is the buyer. Why should he or she choose you above all the other products available?

A bad answer focuses on you: "Because I really need the job," "Because I really want the job," or "Because I would be great at it and love it."

A good answer focuses on them: What problems can you solve for them? What solutions do you provide to them? Tie everything to what they have asked for in a candidate, both in what you read in the job description (job interview preparation is essential to answering this question) and what you learned through asking questions in the interview (if you've had a chance to do that yet).

Think about the things a hiring manager is looking for: the skill sets, the relationships, the background, the character traits...everything that is necessary to be successful in this role. Maybe it's going to be an incredible amount of work, so you need to point out your work ethic. Maybe it's going to require tremendous communication skills, so you need to give an example of yours. Maybe it requires a quick learning curve, so you can say why you're going to be able to get up to speed quickly. Maybe it requires a particular background, and you have that.

Know how your skill set equals the skill set required for this position, and then deliver a concise but detailed statement that explains that. Show them that you fit. And provide a few examples of how you have done that in the past (which means that you can do it again for them). What have you achieved or accomplished that make you a great fit for this role?

Here's an example: "I'm the best for this because you said you were looking for A, B, and C: I've got A...we talked about that; I've got B...I showed you that; I've got C...you asked me questions about that. I fit all your requirements. That's why I'm the best fit for this position." You are reiterating what you have talked about and summed it up for them.

Don't be shy...tell them why they need you.

Job Interview Question 92

Why do you have a big gap in your employment history?

A gap on your resume can be anxiety-inducing for a job seeker, and for the employer who's looking at them for a potential hire. But it's really not as bad as you think. Actually, many people have employment gaps, and they have them for a lot of reasons ranging from the poor economy and mass layoffs in recent years to family obligations of the sandwich generation.

It's not that big of a deal. You just need an explanation. The company wants you to explain the situation to them in a way that makes sense:

- "I took time to stay home with my children."
- "I took time to be with an ailing parent."
- "I took time to be available for a family member with a terminal illness."
- "I was ill / injured and took time to recover."
- "I was laid off and took time to update my skills by taking X classes." (This is a fantastic use of your time!)

They just want you to explain it to them. Be honest. You never ever want to lie or try to fudge your employment dates. They are very likely to check your references and as soon as they see that you lied, you're chances are gone.

But don't just give an abrupt answer like, "I took time to stay with my mother who died of cancer." Give them a little bit more:

"Unfortunately, my mom was terminal with cancer and I wanted to spend time with her and I had the opportunity to do so. I was the person in the family who was responsible for getting her to and from doctors and taking care of her day-to-day needs. It was a very special time. She's passed now, and I am ready to jump back into my career."

Did you stay home with your kids? Say so: "I was a stay-at-home mom. I raised 4 kids. I have them all in school now and I'm now at a point where I have a lot of time and a lot of energy and a lot of drive and desire to put my skill sets to use in a professional capacity. I think this opportunity is an ideal chance for me to use them to help you _____."

That blank needs to be filled with something like, "drive your profits", "increase your revenue", "decrease your costs", "increase your customers", "decrease your production time", or something that sells you to them as an asset that can help them achieve their goals.

Whatever your reason, be strategic and bring it back around to what can contribute to the company. What skills do you have? What problems can you solve? What benefits do you bring?

Give your explanation, focus on the future, stay positive, and you'll be fine.

Why do you think you can manage a team without any prior managerial experience?

If you're interviewing for your first management-level job, you will definitely be asked some version of this question. They'll want to know if you think you can do this job and why.

The key here is to explain that at some point, everybody who becomes a manager has to manage a team without any prior managerial experience. Everybody who is a successful manager has made that transition. What then, makes you confident that you are someone who can make that transition? What do you have in common with those people so that you can say, "they did it, and this is why I can do it, too."

I would give an answer that sounds something like this: "What I've seen is that a really successful manager is someone who is extremely driven, has a strong work ethic, has strong communication skills, wants the best for the company as well as for their employees, is willing to train and mentor others, and is someone who lifts people up and helps develop them and re- moves obstacles from their success. I am that kind of person and I can give you some examples of that. In X role, I did Y. In A role, I did B." The examples you give should show you exhibiting those character traits in various situations.

Maybe you had a role where you had to make people do things but you had no authority over them. That means that you had to be a better manager than someone with the power to actually make them do something. You had no stick, so you had to use only the carrot. That makes extremely strong managerial experience. If you have a story where you were on a team and took on the role of leader to get the team to a goal, then absolutely tell that story. Tell what obstacles you faced, how you resolved them, and what the results were.

I also like turning the question back to them: "So, Mr. Manager, at some point, you didn't have managerial experience, either, right?" They will agree, of course, because they have to. So you say, "What made you think that you were someone who could take on that role?" They will say, "Because I was A, B, and C." You say, "Well, I'm that way, too, and I can be successful, just as you have been."

This question is also an ideal time to introduce your 30/60/90-day plan. It's extremely helpful at management-level interviews because they demonstrate your strategic thinking and problem-solving skills, both of which are essential to a successful manager. And when you write out your goals, you will show them that you do, in fact, know what it takes to be successful in this job and you are completely capable of it.

Why do you want to join this company?

The hot button question: Why do you want to work here?

All companies want to know that you want to work for them rather than you just want a job. An enthusiastic employee is a better employee—and more pleasant to work with, too.

A good answer to this question should always be part of your job interview prep. Your answer to this question should sound like, "I want to join this company because…" and then you need to list at least 3 reasons why.

The first one should always show fit in terms of professional skills: "…I can see where my skill sets would benefit you in this particular position. Because they would benefit you, I would also benefit personally, professionally, and financially from that. If I can come in here and fix this problem for you, I'm sure you'll have other problems I can fix down the road, and that looks like a great future for me."

This one tells them why you're excited about what you can do for them. It still places the emphasis on what they're getting out of hiring you.

The second one can show fit, but more of a cultural fit: "Another reason I want to join this company is that I like the culture. It fits me. I like what I've been reading about the company, and it seems like a great fit for my personality and values and who I want to be working for."

The more specific you can be in your answer, the better. It is absolutely critical that you do your company research before the interview so that you can give these specific examples. What does this company do that appeals to you? Is it a top company in its field? Are they known for their cutting-edge products? Do they have a great reputation for customer service? Are they known for being a great place to work? Do they emphasize employee development? Talk about those things that speak to you about the company and your fit for it.

And then you can say something that personalizes it a little more, like: "The job is in a great location for me. I've always wanted to move here." Or, "It's only 5 minutes from my house, and I love that." Or, "I've always used these products, and I just love them and am really excited about being a part of that." Something that gives you another reason of your own for wanting this job.

Show them your sincere enthusiasm. All of these reasons give them one more reason to hire you.

Job Interview Question 95

Why do you want to switch from an academic field to business/industry?

The one big perception / misconception about academics is that they can't make it in the 'real' world. They are secure in their ivory towers and not coming out any time soon. So if you find yourself trying to leap from your own ivory tower (or ivory laboratory, as the case may be) your interviewer is going to want to know why. What will you have to say for yourself? This question is an excellent jumping-off point for you to talk about your drive, your enthusiasm, and your ambition. Break the stereotype!

If it were me, I would say something like this: "I want to switch because I want to be rewarded for the things that I do. In an academic field I can work day and night, 24 hours, and no one will notice, and I will not be paid any more than my peers are. In a business role, it's my perception that the harder I work and the more that I do, the more the company will reward me. I'll have even more opportunities to take on more responsibility, which will in turn give me more reward."

What can that reward be? Recognition, money, more authority as you climb the ladder, the opportunity to influence others, the chance to be appreciated for what you do, and even the opportunity to be treated differently based on your success.

Anytime you have something in your background that goes against the norm (a gap in your experience, a side-step off your career path, a job that looks like a demotion, and so on) the interviewer will want to know why. All you have to do is provide a reasonable explanation.

You have the power to tell your story in a way that reflects well on you. In this case, the story shows that you want something more for yourself. You are ambitious and energetic and want to be rewarded for your hard work.

In most cases (including moving from academia to industry), you want to tell the story in a way that makes it clear that you aren't running away from whatever situation you were previously in...you are running TO the situation you want to be in. You're not ever going to talk about how bad it was where you were...you're only going to talk about how excited you are to be moving forward. Keep your story positive.

Job Interview Question 96

Why do you want to work for someone else after owning your own business / freelancing?

LOTS of hiring managers will have a hard time believing that you can start taking orders after being your own boss. It's not a big leap to make...it would be difficult for many people. Your best answer to this difficult job interview question will be honest but positive.

My best answer would sound like this: "I am really good at X, but I'm not good at Y, so I'm ready to move into being part of a company again." X would be whatever technical skill or skill set I have that is going to be required in this job. Y would be whatever business acumen necessary for growing your own business, but not needed in this new job.

As in, "I'm a really good graphic designer, but I'm really not good at getting customers." You can't successfully run a business if you don't have the marketing skill to get customers. But in a larger company, someone else will do that for you. All you have to do is design.

In general, it sounds like this: "I'm better at doing the job than I am at marketing the job, and I wasn't ready to expand and bring other people into my business who could do that for me. What I really want to do is focus on the core skills that I'm very good at. I want the chance to hone them even more and do the things I need to do for an employer in a concentrated fashion. I know that will give me a real sense of achievement, and I know that I will still be financially rewarded for that as a part of this organization."

Another great answer tells them that you're a people person: "I want to be where I can work with others. I'm tired of working by myself all the time. I want to be part of a group, or part of a team."

Or you can keep it simple and say, "I just didn't enjoy self-employment as much as I think you should when you're self-employed. I enjoy being part of a company and having colleagues to learn from, bounce ideas off of, and share the day with."

All of these answers make it clear that it's your choice to come in from the world of self-employment. You're not going to ever talk about how it was a colossal failure, or you can't afford the insurance, or you're about to go bankrupt. You're going to say, "I tried it and decided it was not for me....but this opportunity is."

Job Interview Question 96

Why have you been out of work for so long?

Boy, I bet you'd like to know the answer to that question, too! The job search can be a very difficult time for many people, but it's important that you show a positive face to everyone. Answer every job interview question with as much positivity and as little negativity as you can. It makes you more appealing to others and puts you in a better spot to receive a job offer.

The worst thing you can do is shrug your shoulders and say something vague about the job market. And you can even do better than saying, "I just haven't found the right opportunity yet." It's better to point out that you were out of work by choice.

If you can, talk about how you took some time for some personal things before you hit the job search (maybe because you had a nice severance package, maybe for some other reason). Why would you want to do that? Because it's helpful to you if you can point out that in reality, you haven't actually been in an active job search for as long as it seems.

So that gives you a 3-6 month cushion of time and then you can say, "So I've only really been actively looking for the last 4 months or so, and I've been on some interviews, but nothing that really was a great fit. But it's REALLY picked up lately, so I don't think that I'm going to be in the search for much longer."

Do you see what I'm doing here? So overall, I'm saying, "Well, first, I didn't start it really as soon as I probably should have because I took that time off, and second, the market's been pretty bad, and third, it just takes a couple of months to really get a good search going. The average time from first contact to job offer, if you're going to get one, is 8 weeks, so the fact that I've only been searching for 4 months is probably the biggest factor."

And then, this is a really **big key point**: say that "based on what I'm seeing, though, it's really picking up and I don't expect to be unemployed for much longer." That's an important psychological tactic to use: everybody wants what someone else wants, so give yourself a little bit of that aura of unattainability by pointing out that you are going to be snapped up soon.

http://careerconfidential.com

Job Interview Question 98

Why have you changed jobs so frequently over the past X years?

Job-hopping is not a great habit. When you stay at a job for only a few months or a year, over and over again, you are cultivating an image of someone who can't be depended upon, who doesn't know what they want, and who's probably more than a little immature. Employers question your loyalty, and tend to shy away from hiring you because you look like a very expensive disruption rather than a potentially valuable and stable employee.

Still, there are cases where there are good reasons for job-hopping (or at least where it was no one's fault). If you have a few too many jobs in the last few years on your resume, they're going to ask you about it in the interview. You should have an answer ready to go, and it needs to make sense.

A bad answer is going to reinforce the stereotypes they have about job-hoppers:

"I get bored easily."

"I was chasing the money."

"For some reason, people don't seem to like me."

"I keep ending up in hostile work environments."

"I've had a string of bad luck lately."

"I got fired...over and over again."

All those answers say negative things about you.

A good answer is going to give them a reason that makes sense.

The person who's been laid off should say, "Gosh, I wish I hadn't had to change jobs. It wasn't my choice. With the economy, I was laid off of two different projects, (give a few details). So it's not that I really like it. I wish that hadn't happened, but that's where I find myself now."

"These jobs were contract jobs." (Or other jobs where there wasn't any type of commitment or expectation from the employer.)

"I've been looking for the right position." (The follow up question from them will be, "How do you know this is the right position?" You should be able to give them 3 solid reasons why this position is a great fit for you, professionally, culturally, and personally.)

"The company went out of business."

"Our division was dissolved."

"My spouse is in the military, and we had to move."

All those are good reasons. Some of them show that it wasn't your fault, and if that's true, you should definitely say so. If you can, tell them why your job hopping wasn't a bad thing--talk about what you learned from those experiences that help make you a better-rounded person and a more valuable asset to them as a company.

Job Interview Question 99

Why haven't you been promoted?

If you're someone with quite a bit of experience but you haven't moved up the career ladder, you can expect to be asked why you haven't been promoted. Employers don't worry about this issue quite as much as if you had been fired, but both situations do make them wonder if you have some secret fault they don't know about yet.

Remember that hiring you is a risk because they'll be investing time and money into training you and getting you up to speed in the job. And they really don't want to have to go through this hiring process again. So this question is yet another way to ask about your weaknesses, or otherwise uncover flaws while they still have the chance.

The best answer is one where you can say, "I was actually offered a promotion, but I wasn't interested. I didn't want to take on that additional responsibility." There could be a lot of reasons for this. Maybe you had small children or other family obligations. Maybe you had something else going on.

Or, "I was offered a promotion, but I wasn't interested in taking on that role." Maybe you just weren't interested in the responsibilities of that job.

Or, "I wanted to move in a different direction in the company. The promotions that were offered to me (or available to me) were going to take me in a direction I didn't want to go." Not every job you qualify for is going to fit neatly into the career path you are following.

All of these answers tell the best story you can tell, which is that it was your choice.

Or, it could be that the lack of promotional opportunities in your old company is exactly why you're in the job search. Maybe you worked for a small company with no room for you to grow and develop. Then it makes perfect sense for you to be looking for advancement opportunities in another organization.

What you don't want to do is give the impression that you're lazy and didn't want to do the work; that you weren't offered a promotion because you're not good at your job; or that you don't have the work ethic or the people skills necessary to move up the chain.

One thing that will help you in this situation or any situation where there's some question about your background: your references. A great reference will counter a lot of doubts the hiring manager has about you. Cultivate good references and prep them before your interview.

http://careerconfidential.com

Job Interview Question 100

Why should we give you the job over the other candidates?

This is a tough question. Most people are not that comfortable with the idea of tooting their own horn, but that's exactly what you have to do here. So feel free to brag. They're looking for you to sell yourself for the job. Tell them why they need you.

In order to do that, you have to have done your pre-interview research plus a little self-analysis. Know how your skill set equals the skill set required for this position...and if you can, show how you offer that PLUS a bit more. That little bit extra is helpful to give you the edge over other candidates.

You don't need a lot, just one more thing that makes you special over and above the other candidates. Say what that is and how it's going to help you exceed their expectations for that role. You won't just meet them, you'll exceed them. Talk about one or two specific accomplishments that really highlight you as a great candidate for this role. Talk about how well you fit culturally with the company, and how they're going to see that even more when they talk to your references. (And your references better be outstanding...make sure you prep your references before the interview. Just give them a heads up that you're interviewing and what the job is for and what particular skills or accomplishments would be helpful for them to talk about.)

Everything you talk about should be focused on how you're going to not just meet, but exceed their expectations.

Say something like, "I deserve the job because I have the skills, I meet the qualifications, I fit you culturally, I've done the work before successfully, I'm going to be able to perform successfully in this role, and that's what you want, do you agree?"

It's OK to ask if they agree or if you've answered the question—you need to know if you answered what they were asking, and they deserve an answer to an issue for them. It's easy. Just say, "Do you agree?" or "did that answer your question?" or "did I answer your question completely?" That's just good communication skills that are necessary in a job interview situation.

Job Interview Question 101

Why would you accept a lesser salary than what you made before?
Won't you jump ship when a better offer comes along?

You might very well come across a better opportunity in the future, but now is not the time to talk about it. Now is the time to alleviate the concerns of that hiring manager so that they feel comfortable pulling the trigger to make you an offer!

Your best answer is to say something like this:

"If I take the job with you, I'm not going to just be taking it for the money. I'm looking at the whole picture. I'm interested in more than just the paycheck. I'm interested in the quality of the company, the quality of my work life, the caliber of my manager, the healthcare and other benefits, the unique things that this company has that other companies don't.

Another company could come along and offer me more money...that could happen no matter what. That's not really relevant because I don't take a job just because of the money, I take a job because of all those factors as a whole. I need a job that will meet all my needs. When I look at this job with you, I see a job that will meet all my needs.

Do I want to be paid as highly as I can be for the work that I do? Yes, of course. But if I commit to you for this job, I will be committed and I won't be spending my time looking for a so-called better offer. I will be working hard and performing and exceeding for you.

I don't sign on for short term jobs. You can look at my history. I've been with XYZ organization for a number of years. I won't take a job with an organization that I'm not committed to."

If they've asked you this question, they like you a lot and they're wondering if you're too good to be true. So all you have to do is put their fears to rest by trying to take the money question out of it, or by at least minimizing it as much as possible.

Additional Resource Guide

Visit Career Confidential (http://careerconfidential.com) to find blog articles, videos, free resources and guaranteed tools to help you get hired fast.

Read More On…

Brag Books - http://careerconfidential.com/brag-book-essentials-for-every-job-hunter/

30-60-90-Day Plans - http://careerconfidential.com/creating-a-30-60-90-day-plan-that-wins-the-job-offer/

Free Training Webinars

Career Confidential offers online training sessions to arm you with smart, in-sightful, cutting-edge tips and strategies for your resume, job search, and interviews. http://careerconfidential.com/training-webinars/

Free Podcast – How to Write a Cover Letter - http://careerconfidential.com/specials/podcast-pick/

Free Apps for iPhone, iPad and Android

Job Interview Questions and Answers- Free interactive

video app. http://jobinterviewquestionsandanswersapp.com/

Resume Review Pro - Improve your resume in less

than 10 minutes. http://resumereviewproapp.com/

Job Search Tips- Comprehensive app gives you a

strong resume, attention-getting cover letters, and

more interviews.   http://jobsearchtipsapp.com/

More eBooks by Peggy McKee on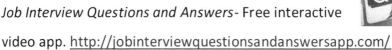

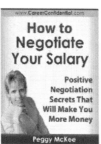
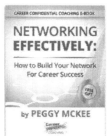

http://careerconfidential.com

Made in the USA
Middletown, DE
27 October 2017